Marat Khairulin

RUSSIAN AVIATION COLOURS 1909–1922 Book IV

STRATUS

STRATUS sp.j.
Po. Box 123,
27-600 Sandomierz 1, Poland
e-mail: office@mmpbooks.biz
as
Mushroom Model Publications,
3 Gloucester Close, Petersfield, Hampshire GU32 3AX, UK. E-mail: rogerw@mmpbooks.biz
http://www.mmpbooks.biz
Originally published as:
КРАСКИ РУССКОЙ АВИАЦИИ 1909–1922 гг. Книга I
© Фонд «Русские Витязи» 2015
© STRATUS 2018
© MMPBooks 2018
ISBN 978-83-65281-98-2

All rights reserved. No part of this publication may be reproduced, stored in a retrieval system, or transmitted in any form or by any means, electronic, mechanical, photocopying, recording or otherwise without the prior permission of MMPBooks.

British Library Cataloguing in Publication Data:
A catalogue record for this book is available from the British Library.

Editor in chief

Roger Wallsgrove

Editorial Team

Bartłomiej Belcarz
Artur Juszczak
Robert Pęczkowski

Layout concept	Artur Juszczak
Cover	Artur Juszczak
DTP	Stratus sp.j.
Colour Drawings	A. V. Kazakov
Translation	Wojtek Matusiak
Edited by	Roger Wallsgrove

Printed by
Drukarnia Diecezjalna
Sandomierz
Poland

Table of Contents

Acknowledgements 4

Part IV Against Soviets 5

6TH CHAPTER AIR FORCES OF THE WHITE ARMIES 5

Pilot 5

Aviation of the Armed Forces in the South of Russia 6

    The Volunteer Army 6

    Naval Aviation of the Volunteer Army 17

    Almighty Don Host 19

    Kuban' Cossack Host 34

    Forces of the Trans-Caspian Region 44

Aviation of the Russian Army 45

Aviation of the North-Western Army 63

Aviation of the Western Volunteer Army 67

Aviation of the White forces in the North of Russia 76

    Slavo-British Aviation Corps 76

    Murmansk Aviation Divizion 81

    1st Aviation Otryad of the Northern Front 88

Aviation of the White forces in the East of Russia 89

    People's Army 89

    The armed forces of the All-Russian Government (admiral A. V. Kolchak's) 97

    Armed forces of the Russian Eastern Periphery (of ataman G. V. Semënov) 120

Acknowledgements

The author considers it his duty to express gratitude to everyone who assisted him in working on the book. The following persons have contributed invaluably by providing material from their private collections: M. Blinov, T. Kitvel', G. F. Petrov, M. S. Selivanov and A. A. Zarayskiy.

The author wishes to thank particularly the following persons for their assistance in working on the book: A. O. Aleksandrov, S. G. Alekseyev, K. Babro, M. Bukhman, Z. Čejka, M. I. Ivkov, A. V. Kibovskiy, A. M. Kirindas, V. P. Kulikov, A. A. Litvin, N. G. Malyshev, M. S. Neshkin, G. Ramoshka, R. Rimmel, I. L. Ryzhov, V. K. Spatarel' and Ye. A. Ushakov.

The author is very grateful to all those who have provided material from family archives: M. F. Ivkov, S. V. Kharchev and N. P. Tikhomirov.

This book would not have been possible without drawings of A. V. Kazakov, who carried the burden of work on the 'colour', and without the help of T. A. Shtyk, who has drawn several complex emblems and the beautiful cover artwork.

It would also have been impossible to create the book without the help of staff at the following archives, museums and libraries: State Archive of the Russian Federation (SAotRF; Gosudarstvennyy arkhiv Rossiyskoy Federatsii, GARF), Russian State Military Historical Archive (RSMHA; Rossiyskiy gosudarstvennyy voyenno-istoricheskiy arkhiv, RGVIA), Russian State Military Archive (RSMH; Rossiyskiy gosudarstvennyy voyennyy arkhiv, RGVA), Russian State Archive of the Navy (RSAotN; Rossiyskiy gosudarstvennyy arkhiv voyenno-morskogo flota, RGAVMF), Russian State Library (RSL; Rossiyskaya gosudarstvennaya biblioteka, RGB), Russian State Art Library (RSAL; Rossiyskaya gosudarstvennaya biblioteka iskusstv, RGBI), Central Armed Forces Museum (CAFM; Tsentral'nyy muzey Vooruzhënnykh Sil, TsMVS), Central Naval Museum (CNM; Tsentral'nyy voyenno-morskiy muzey, TsVMM), Central House of Aviation and Astronautics (CHoA&A; Tsentral'nyy dom aviatsii i kosmonavtiki, TsDAiK), DeGolyer Library (SMU), Eesti Rahvusarhiiv, Kara muzejs, National Air and Space Museum (NASM).

The author offers many thanks to the employees of the 'Russian Knights' ('Russkiye Vityazi') Aviation Assistance Foundation for their patience: V. I. Iz"yurov, Yu. V. Khamzina, O. G. Leonov, L. A. Navdayeva and Yu. M. Zheltonogin.

Part IV
Against Soviets

6ᵀᴴ CHAPTER
AIR FORCES OF THE WHITE ARMIES

PILOT

Like a sky-reaching falcon,
A biplane is flying in the air,
Leaving the cramped world below,
Cutting the fog around

Young, brave pilot,
Warrior from head to foot,
He is a bomber and a machine gunner,
A faithful companion to Moscow…

He strikes the adversary in flight
Like a mighty thunder,
Lighting the darkness
From the sky-high blue fall.

And to his native soldiers
Opens the path in battle,
To quickly hit the chests of
Fierce enemies…

Like a sky-reaching falcon,
A biplane is flying in the air,
The wonderful victory laurel
Will soon, soon be given to us!..[1]

This part will examine in detail the recognition and national markings, as well as the emblems, of the air force of the White formations in the south, northwest, west, north and east of Russia.

---
1 The poem "Pilot" was published with the author's note "brother of an officer" in the Arkhangel'sk newspaper "Vestnik Vremennogo Pravitel'stva Severnoy Oblasti" ("Journal of the Temporary Government of the Northern Region") No. 155 of 17 July 1919.

Aviation of the Armed Forces in the South of Russia

The Armed Forces in the South of Russia (AFSR) were established on 8 January 1919[2], after the signing of an agreement between the Commander of the Volunteer Army and the atamans of the Almighty Don Host and the Kuban' Cossack Host to unite all land and sea forces operating in the south of Russia against the Bolsheviks. General A. I. Denikin became the General Commander of the AFSR. It should be noted that the history of the White air force units predated their incorporation into the AFSR, commencing back in 1918, as will be discussed below.

The Volunteer Army

The air forces in the south of Russia began to be formed at the beginning of 1918, thanks to the equipment that had earlier belonged to the Russian Air Force and had been evacuated from Ukraine. Some of the aeroplanes had flown over from the Reds. The process of forming the Aviation of the Volunteer and Don Armies proceeded with great difficulty. Throughout 1918 only five aviation otryads were formed in the Volunteer Army, and only two each in the Don and Astrakhan' armies.[3]

The 1st Aviation Otryad had been formed at Rostov-na-Donu by 8 May of the same year on the basis of the orders of *polkovnik* Drozdovskiy, the Commander of the 1st Brigade of Russian Volunteers, of 20 April 1918.

The first aeroplanes of the otryad, Voisin type, were received from the Lebedev plant at Taganrog. Other aviation otryads of the Volunteer Army were formed at Yekaterinodar, the 2nd on 1 August 1918, and the 3rd, 4th and 5th in the autumn. The aviation park at Simferopol' joined the Volunteer Army in December.

According to the establishment, each otryad was to receive six machines, but this almost never happened as there were not enough machines. Available ones were extremely worn out and were often under repair. The aeroplanes had served in the Great War, 1915–1917, they had flown actively on the Austro-German front and had been overhauled more than once.

As a rule, all the aeroplanes of the Volunteer Army displayed on their fabric covering the old 'tsar's' markings: roundels in Russian colours. It is common knowledge that the White movement had its own flag, white-blue-red, the old Russian national one. So the volunteers did not have to replace the old markings with new insignia.

In the archival documents of the White formations, no mention was made of new recognition markings of the army aviation, nor of any otryad or personal emblems.

In the rare photographs of the Civil War period, aeroplanes of the volunteers can be mistaken for machines of the First World War Russian army.

From May 1919 the White armies in the south of Russia started to receive deliveries from the allies (from Britain). Some of the machines were transferred to the Volunteer Army by the British through the RAF South Russia Instructional Mission, from Nos. 47 and 221 Squadrons RAF[4]. In total, during 1919 the AFSR aviation received about 200 aeroplanes of various types, mainly the obsolete R.E.8 two-seater reconnaissance aircraft (100 machines), as well as the de Havilland DH.9 (about 60), Sopwith Camel (about 30) and S.E.5 (8). Therefore, from the summer of 1919, the 'new' British types prevailed in the AFSR aviation over the old French ones (Nieuport, Farman and Voisin).

A lot has been published about the actions of British air units during the Civil War on Russian territory, not only in the West, but also in Russia.[5]

We include here just a few examples of photographs and colour schemes of the most famous aeroplanes of the British that operated against the Red Army.

The Allies 'generously' supplied the AFSR aviation, delivering their fairly battered and old machines to it.

Airmen of the 5th Aviation Otryad of the Volunteer Army, serving in the Caucasus at Grozny, were the first to receive British aeroplanes. In early May 1919 No. 221 Squadron based at Petrovsk handed

---

2   Here and further in the text up to the "Aviation of the North-Western Army" chapter, the dates are given according to the old style (Julian calendar).
3   The aviation of the Almighty Don Host will be discussed below.
4   John T. Smith. "Gone to Russia to Fight. The RAF in South Russia 1918–1920". Amberley Publishing. UK. 2010. P. 195.
5   See the articles published in the "Vestnik Vozdushnogo Flota" ("Journal of the Air Force") magazine: "Angliyskaya aviatsiya v bor'be protiv Sovetskoy Rossii" ("English aviation in combat against the Soviet Russia"), No. 1–2/1921, pp. 32–33; G. Jones "47 otryad korolevskikh vozdushnykh sil na Yuge Rossii" ("47 Squadron RAF in the South of Russia") No. 4–5/1924, pp. 7–12.

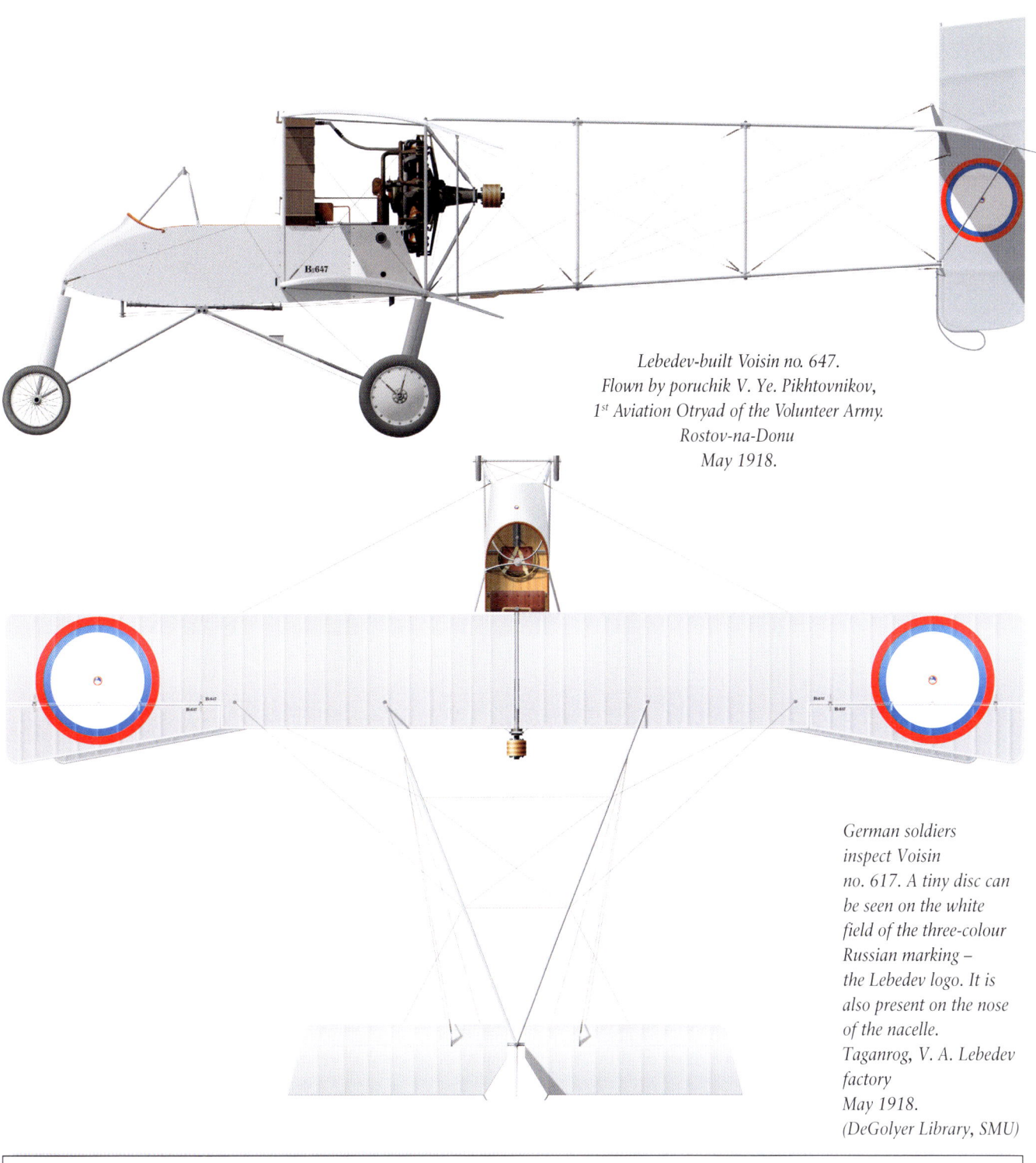

*Lebedev-built Voisin no. 647.
Flown by poruchik V. Ye. Pikhtovnikov,
1st Aviation Otryad of the Volunteer Army.
Rostov-na-Donu
May 1918.*

*German soldiers
inspect Voisin
no. 617. A tiny disc can
be seen on the white
field of the three-colour
Russian marking –
the Lebedev logo. It is
also present on the nose
of the nacelle.
Taganrog, V. A. Lebedev
factory
May 1918.
(DeGolyer Library, SMU)*

Nieuport 21 fighter with 'Tsar's' markings. Tsaritsyn front Summer 1919. (GA RF)

Morane-Parasol aeroplanes of an aviation otryad of the Volunteer Army. The machine on the right was built at Duks factory, as shown by the roundels with white outline on the wings. 1919. (GA RF)

Sopwith Camel serial no. F1955. Flown by Captain S. M. Kinkead, No. 47 Squadron RAF, 'B' Flight. Flying this machine on 30 September 1919 Kinkead scored a victory over a Nieuport of D. V. Shchekin, Red military pilot from the 47th Aviation Otryad.

Sopwith Camel fighters before despatch to the front line to Beketovka. No. 47 Squadron RAF, 'A' Flight. Yekaterinodar, September 1919. (TsDAiK)

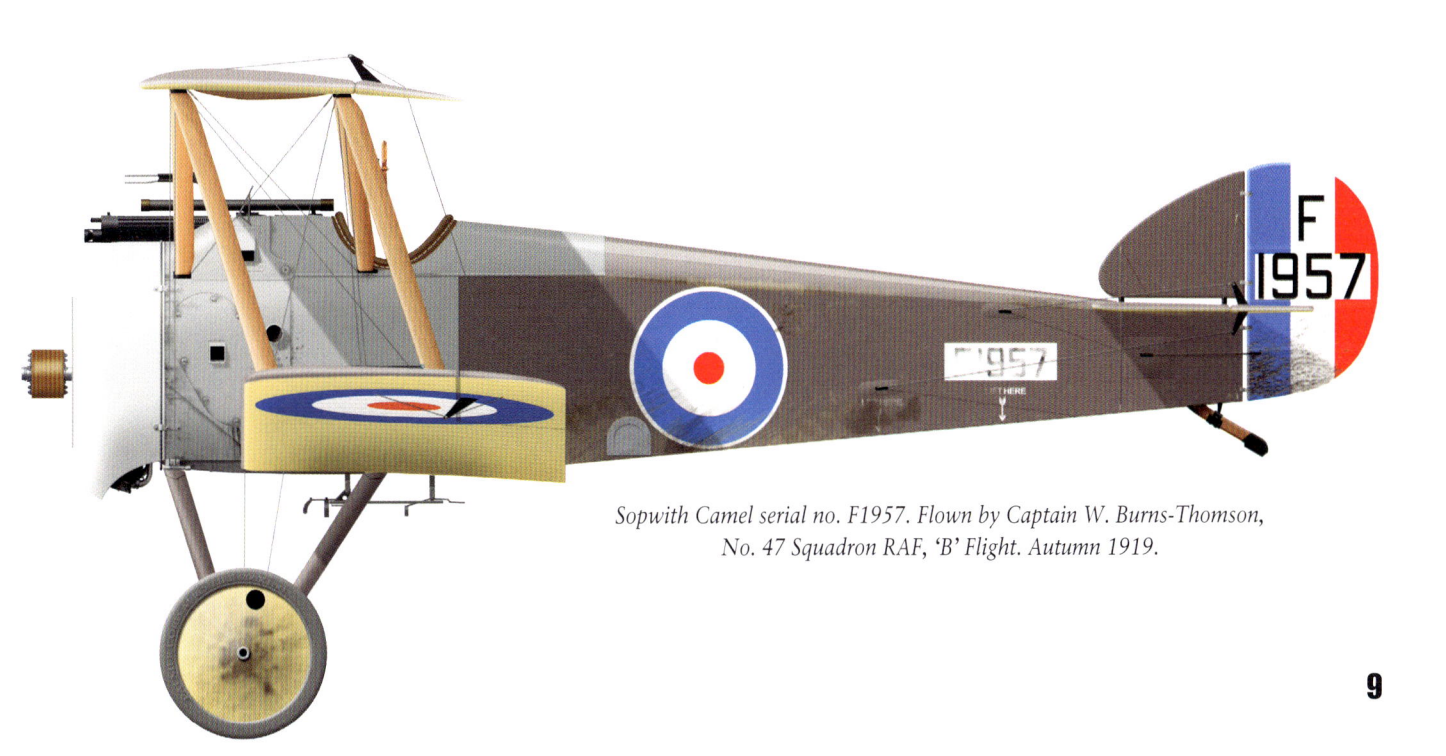

Sopwith Camel serial no. F1957. Flown by Captain W. Burns-Thomson, No. 47 Squadron RAF, 'B' Flight. Autumn 1919.

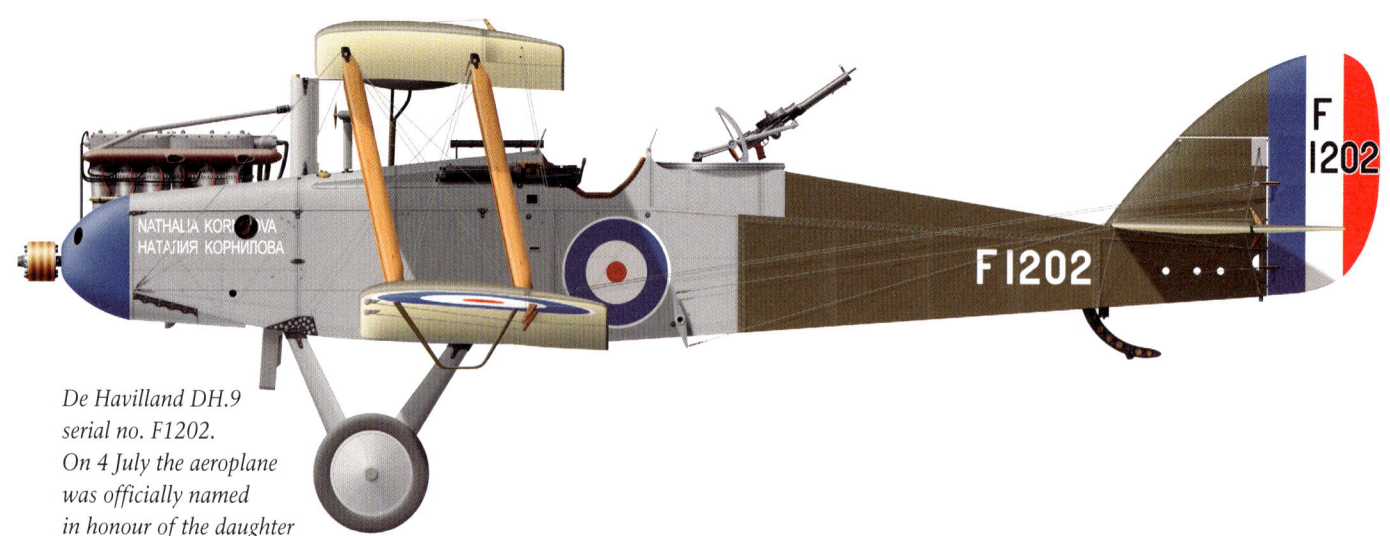

De Havilland DH.9 serial no. F1202. On 4 July the aeroplane was officially named in honour of the daughter of the Russian General Kornilov in the presence of Colonel Maund and the officers of No. 47 Squadron. The inscription "Natalia Kornilova/Natal'ya Kornilova" was applied on its side. This machine was flown in combat by 'C' Flight members, Captains Frogley and Anderson.

De Havillands with Puma engines of No. 47 Squadron at Yekaterinodar airfield. Summer 1919.

Aeroplanes of No. 47 Squadron RAF. From the of spring 1920 the de Havillands, with serial nos. E8987 and E8994, fought with the 5th Aviation Otryad of the Russian Army. The photo was taken at Yekaterinodar airfield in the autumn of 1919. (TsDAiK)

De Havilland serial no. D2854, No. 221 Squadron RAF. Petrovsk winter 1918/1919.

De Havilland serial no. D2842, transferred to the White aviation from No. 47 Squadron in the autumn of 1919. After the defeat of Vrangel' this machine was captured by the Reds and was used in 1921 in the aviation of the 1st Horse Army.

De Havilland serial no. D2842, transferred to the White aviation from No. 47 Squadron in the autumn of 1919. After the defeat of Vrangel' this machine was captured by the Reds and was used in 1921 in the aviation of the 1st Horse Army.

Sopwith Camel serial no. F1954.
6th Aviation Otryad of the Volunteer Army.
Belgorod
August 1919.

Insignia of the assault units. (From the collection of M. S. Selivanov)

Officers of one of the Kornilov assault regiments. Kharkiv. Summer 1919. (From the collection of A. A. Zarayskiy)

Insignia of the assault units. (From the collection of M. S. Selivanov)

12

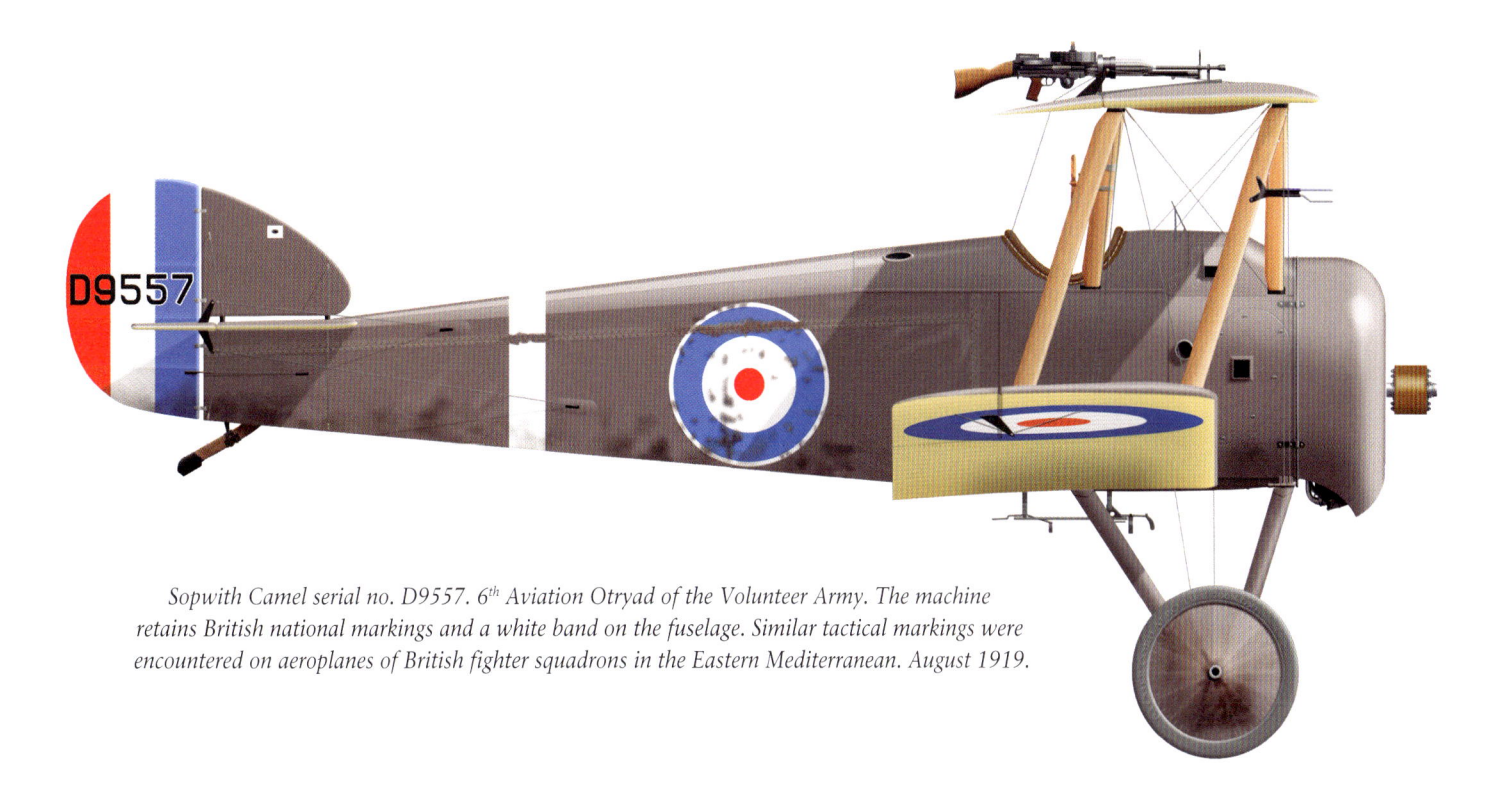

Sopwith Camel serial no. D9557. 6th Aviation Otryad of the Volunteer Army. The machine retains British national markings and a white band on the fuselage. Similar tactical markings were encountered on aeroplanes of British fighter squadrons in the Eastern Mediterranean. August 1919.

Personnel of the 6th Aviation Otryad of the Volunteer Army with their Sopwith Camel fighters. Standing ninth right is military pilot kornet K. K. Artseulov. The picture shows four of the eight aeroplanes of the otryad. Belgorod, August 1919. (GA RF)

two de Havilland DH.9s over to the otryad. General-mayor Kravtsevich, the AFSR inspector of aviation, upon learning about this, sent a telegram to the commander of the otryad, *poruchik* Zabudskoy:

> *Leave one aeroplane in the otryad, transfer the other to the recipient of the first aviation otryad to establish communication with the Eastern Front"*[6]. Receiving no answer, the head of the White Aviation again sent a telegram: "I ask you not to force me to repeat orders, keep one of the overhauled English aeroplanes for yourselves, I order that the other is to be handed over immediately to the receiving officer of the 1st Aviation Otryad. no. 6044. 17 May"[7]. In a telegram to Kravtsevich, the Chief of Staff of the Terek-Dagestan kray forces, general-mayor Maslovskiy, involuntarily revealed the generous policy of the Allies regarding the transfer of their machines: "The English aviation unit at Petrovsk is re-equipped with new aeroplanes. Their old aeroplanes are inactive, and according to available information the Englishmen will willingly give these aircraft to the 5th Aviation Otryad, which is at my disposal, having old [machines] worn-out by uninterrupted heavy work. I think personally that the personnel of the 5th Aviation Otryad is brilliant and able to still bring great benefits with better basis. I ask you to send a telegram to the English HQ at Petrovsk, with a request to give 4 or 5 Hevillends [sic!] to the 5th Aviation Otryad. I am sure that the English will fulfil your request. 14/V.1919. Pyatigorsk*[8].

---

6   RGVA. F. 39540. Op. 1. D. 260. L. 22.
7   Ibid, l. 30.
8   Ibid, l. 44.

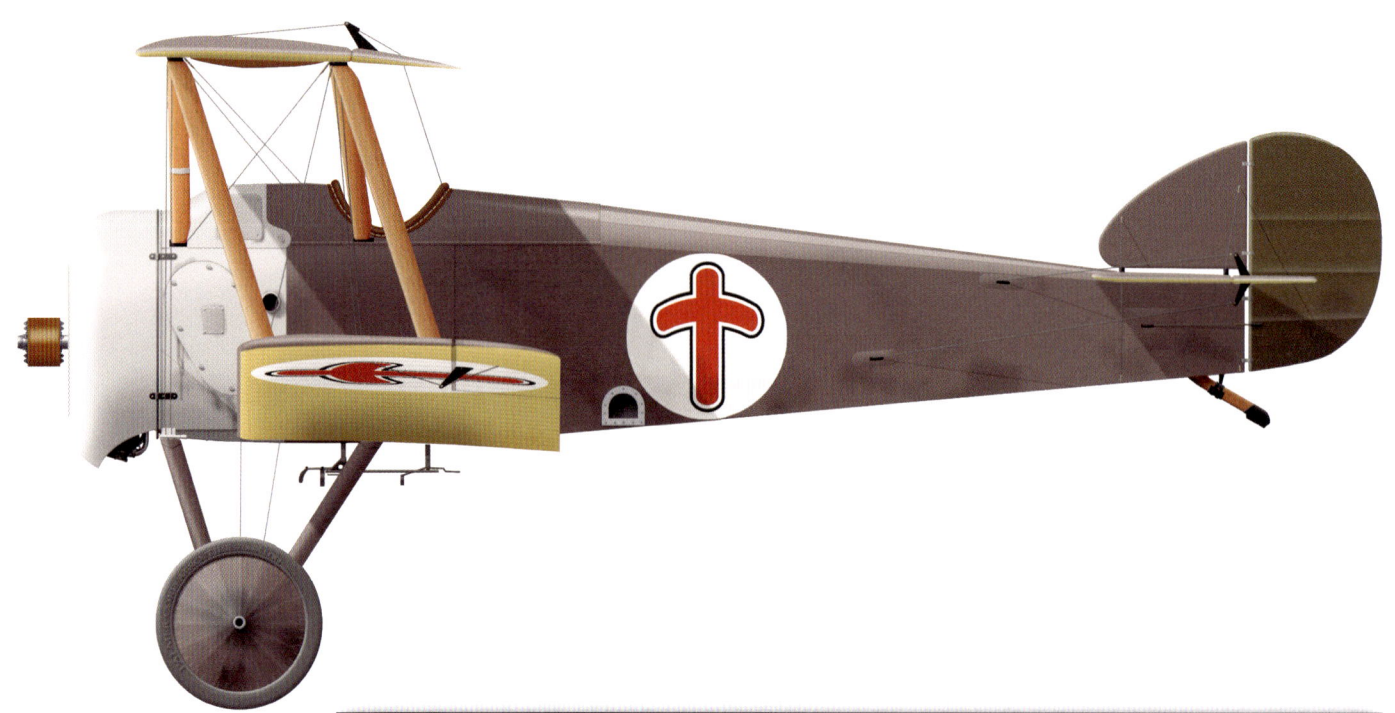

Sopwith Camel with recognition markings of the Georgian air force. The machine was earlier used by the 6th Aviation Otryad of the Volunteer Army.
Tbilisi 1921.
(TsDAiK)

Crash of a Georgian Camel, a rare variant (2F.1). The 6th Aviation Otryad of the Volunteer Army used one such machine, serial no. N6804.
Tbilisi, 1920.
(TsDAiK)

14

LVG C.V no. 14599. Flown by the commander of the 3rd Aviation Divizion of the Volunteer Army, military pilot polkovnik M. Ye. Gartman (Hartmann), March – October 1919. The photos refer to August, when the machine was undergoing repairs at the 1st Aviation Park in Simferopol. (RGB NIOR)

Following the 5th, the 1st Otryad 'general Alekseyev' also re-equipped with de Havilland DH.9s, moving to the front line in June 1919.

Meanwhile, at Yekaterinodar, training of pilots, previously unfamiliar with British equipment, continued at an accelerated pace. The otryads received the 'new' types of machines: R.E.8s (the 3rd, 4th and 9th), Camels (the 6th) and de Havilland DH.9s (the 2nd). Anyway, compared to the old and worn-out machines of the recent war period, the 'English' ones were much better.

The aircraft obtained from the Allies were, of course, adorned with their own, 'native' recognition markings, as well as squadron tactical insignia (numbers, letters or emblems).

A unique photo of machines of the 6th Aviation Otryad of the Volunteer Army, taken at Belgorod during the offensive of Denikin's troops towards Moscow, is illustrative. For example, one of the machines shows clearly a white stripe. All machines display British national markings and serial numbers.

Another machine, serial no. F1954, had its British three-colour roundel replaced by a skull with bones, similar to the emblem of the Kornilov troops. The 6th Otryad was sent to Kharkiv in July, and from there, along with the 1st Army Corps of general-leytenant Kutepov, it advanced towards Moscow. The corps included the Kornilov Assault Brigade (from October, Kornilov Assault Division). The emblem of the Kornilov troops (and other 'death' assault units) has been widely known since 1917.

Several Camel units flew to Georgia in early 1920. The pilots were released, and the aeroplanes remained in the local air force. The ex-British aeroplanes, used by the volunteers, now flew with the crosses of St Nino.

The Aviation Park of the Volunteer Army was formed in December 1918 at Yekaterinodar (slightly later renamed the 1st – after the 2nd Park was formed in Odessa). In February 1919 the 1st Aviation Park moved to Simferopol', taking over the premises of the former A. A. Anatra plant. During 1918–1920 the park overhauled a total of at least 120 machines.

In late July/early August 1919 the park overhauled the German LVG biplane of *polkovnik* Gartman (Hartmann), commanding the 3rd Aviation Divizion of the Volunteer Army. It featured three-colour roundels in Russian colours (on the rudder and wings), and a white-blue-red band around the fuselage. On its side there was also the old German number 14599 and the park marking: "No. 45, 1st Av. P.". The volunteers' chevron was applied closer to the tail, this being the only known case of its use on a land-based aeroplane.[9]

Besides the well-known fact that troops of the Volunteer Army wore chevrons on the left sleeve, the three-colour 'V' was also painted on AFSR armoured trains, armoured cars and other motor vehicles.

Heavy armoured train of the Volunteer Army "For United Russia". The photo was taken in 1919 during the battles for Tsaritsyn. (GA RF)

---

9   The chevrons were applied on machines of the naval aviation, as will be discussed in the next section.

Naval Aviation of the Volunteer Army

The Volunteer Army had relatively few, and poorly armed, naval aviation otryads in the Black and Caspian Seas. These otryads reported in operational terms to local HQs, and in terms of logistics they tried to get everything that was possible to obtain both from the central and district authorities. One can say with certainty that the battle-worthy core was made up of Russian naval aeroplanes that had remained in Sebastopol from 1917, and of German and Austro-Hungarian machines abandoned by the occupants when they left Crimea and Odessa at the end of 1918.[10] Judging by the photographs that depict the ex-German hydroplanes, the aircraft of the Volunteer Army had standard recognition markings. Three-colour roundels in the national colours of Russia with a white edge were applied on the rudder and main planes, and the volunteers' chevron was sometimes present on the fuselage.

Friedrichshafen FF49 hydroplane of the Naval Hydro-Aviation Otryad of the Volunteer Army. On the fuselage, the volunteer's chevron, and on the rudder, fuselage and wings three-colour roundels with a white outline. Nakhimova bay Sevastopol, 1919. (GA RF)

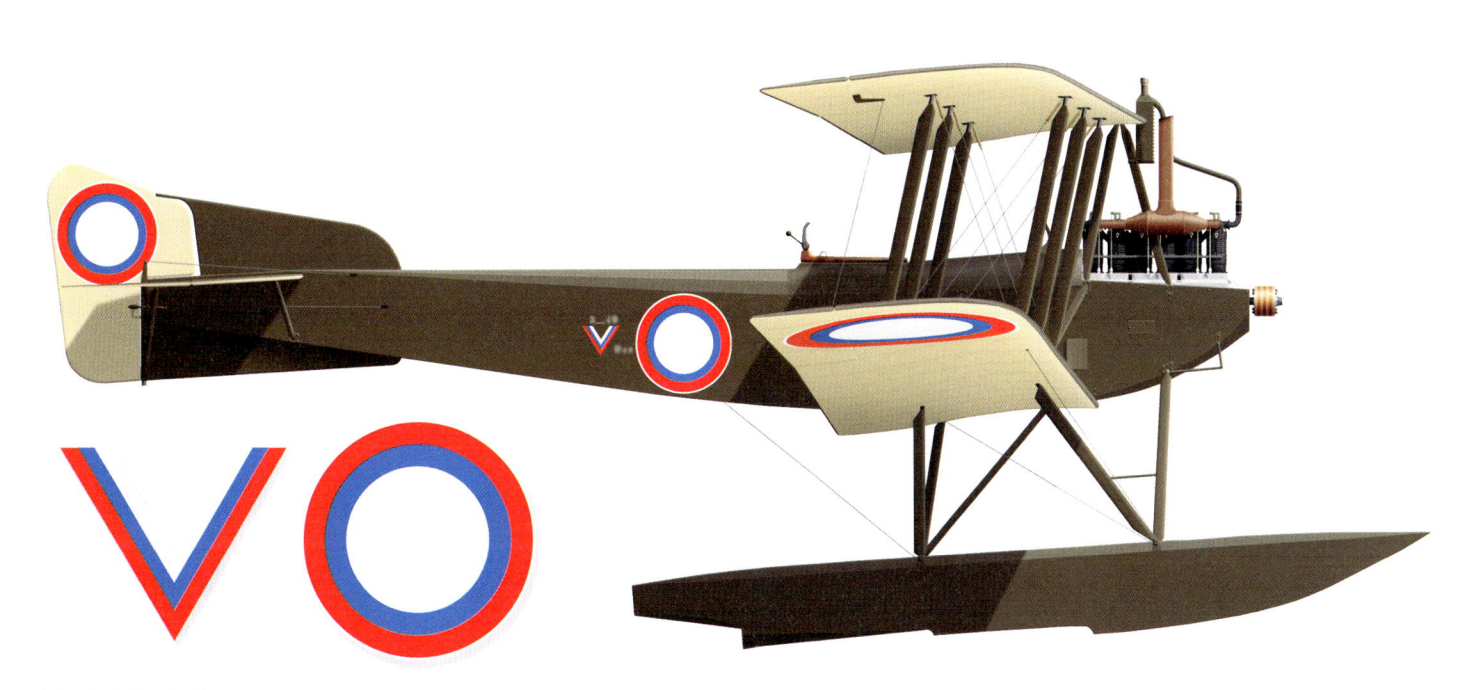

---

10   For more details on the history of AFSR hydro-aviation see the following publications: Alexandrov Andrei. "Abandoned in the Black sea. German and Austro-Hungarian marine aircraft at Sevastopol and Odessa in 1919", "Windsock International" magazine, Vol. 7, No. 1, 1997. pp. 22–25 and Aleksandrov A. O. "Pobedy. Poteri… Zadachi, podrazdeleniya, nachal'stvuyushchiy sostav, letatel'nyye apparaty i vooruzheniye morskoy aviatsii i vozdukhoplavaniya Rossii, a takzhe spisok pobed i poter' s 1894-go po 1920 g." ("Victories, losses… Tasks, units, commanding staff, aircraft and armament of the naval aviation and aeronautics of Russia, and the listing of victories and losses 1894–1920") – SPb.: "IP Kompleks", 2000

*Officers with
a Friedrichshafen
with Russian recognition
markings.
Nakhimova bay
Sevastopol, 1919.
(From the collection
of T. Darcy)*

*Two Friedrichshafens
and an M-5 flying boat.
On the former German
machine the three-colour
roundels can be seen only
on the wings and rudder.
Also the chevron
on the side is missing.
Black Sea
1919 or 1920.*

Sablatnig SF 5 with three-colour roundels of the Volunteer Army on the wings and a chevron on the side. (From the collection of G. Vudmen)

Almighty Don Host

The idea of creating their own air force was first announced at a meeting of the Military Authorities at Novocherkassk, when the report "on the organisation of the Aviation otryad of the Don Host" was received on 11 December 1917.

On 19 January 1918 the Military Authorities approved the report and allocated 89,500 roubles for initial expenses and 90,000 roubles for the support of personnel.

The Don troops captured their first two Voisins directly from under the nose of the Bolsheviks, at the V. A. Lebedev factory at Taganrog; *poruchik* Pavlov and *leytenant* Krygin flew these to Novocherkassk.[11]

However, the creation of the Don aviation advanced slowly. In February 1918 the Bolsheviks captured Novocherkassk, which then was not liberated until late April.

The Don troops recovered two of their unserviceable aeroplanes that had remained in the city, and managed to assemble a single airworthy one from these. The first combat sortie on the Chir front was flown 29 May.

Untiring work continued to find and re-assemble aeroplanes, obtain petrol, oil and other materials, as well as to assemble personnel for the nascent otryad.

11 For more details on the most interesting history of the Don aviation see: "Neizvestnyye vospominaniya V. G. Baranova ob aviatsii na Donu" ("Unknown memoirs of V. G. Baranov about the aviation on the Don"), published in the "Rossiyskiy arkhiv" almanac, 2009 (18th issue), p. 497–556.

Assets that allowed assembling and delivering two more aeroplanes were found partly at Rostov and partly at Taganrog. Valuable military equipment was also coming from Ukraine.

Thus, by August 1918, the Don Aeroplane Otryad had been formed.

The orders about the recognition markings of the young Don aviation were issued on 28 June 1918 and published in the "Donskoy kray" ("Don Country") journal.

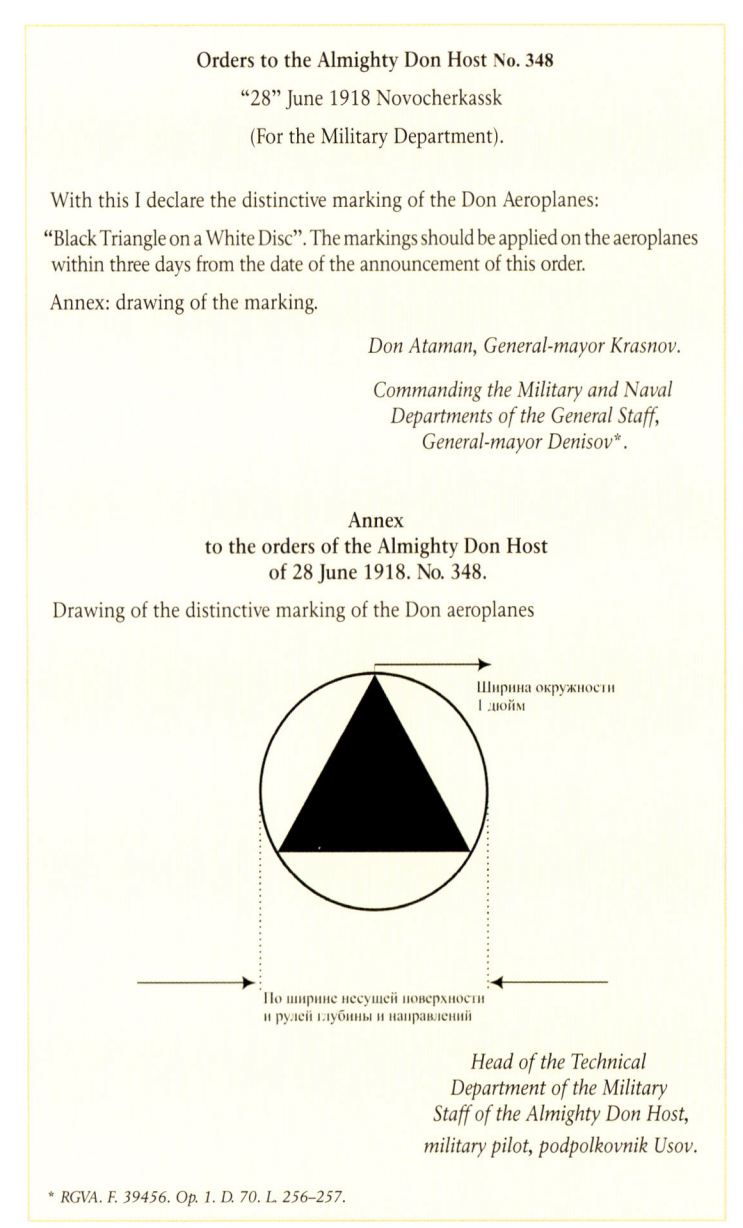

> **Orders to the Almighty Don Host No. 348**
>
> "28" June 1918 Novocherkassk
>
> (For the Military Department).
>
> With this I declare the distinctive marking of the Don Aeroplanes:
>
> "Black Triangle on a White Disc". The markings should be applied on the aeroplanes within three days from the date of the announcement of this order.
>
> Annex: drawing of the marking.
>
> *Don Ataman, General-mayor Krasnov.*
>
> *Commanding the Military and Naval Departments of the General Staff, General-mayor Denisov*.*
>
> **Annex**
> **to the orders of the Almighty Don Host**
> **of 28 June 1918. No. 348.**
>
> Drawing of the distinctive marking of the Don aeroplanes
>
> *Head of the Technical Department of the Military Staff of the Almighty Don Host, military pilot, podpolkovnik Usov.*
>
> * RGVA. F. 39456. Op. 1. D. 70. L. 256–257.

Orders to Almighty Don Host no. 348 of 28 June 1918, published in Novocherkassk newspaper "Donskoy kray" no. 61 of 4 July 1918.

So far, no explanation has been found for why the Don troops chose the black triangle as the recognition marking for their aeroplanes, and also for their armoured cars. Like the point of the compass, showing north – the direction of the attack on the stronghold of Bolshevism, towards Moscow. Perhaps the black triangle on a white background was simply considered a prominent marking. One way or another, the old Russian national markings, the three-colour roundels, were not used by the Don aviation, even though the rare photos do show them, and this will be discussed further. Don troops even used the word 'aeroplane', rather than 'aviation' in the names of their otryads and divizions, obviously attempting to differ from the units of the Volunteer Army.

The first image of the Don national markings can be seen in the photographs from late summer/early autumn 1918 at Novocherkassk. The designation V-6 (В-6) can be seen on the nacelle of one of the machines: the ordinal number of the Voisin aeroplane in the Don aviation. The digit 3 was applied on the rudder of another machine.

General-mayor Krasnov, the Don ataman, wrote in his orders no. 5 of 5 May 1918 that "*permanent army is being formed in the following composition: … z) Don Aeroplane Divizion*". It took almost four months until this plan came true. On 31 August the Don aeroplane otryad was expanded into two otryads (the first and the second).

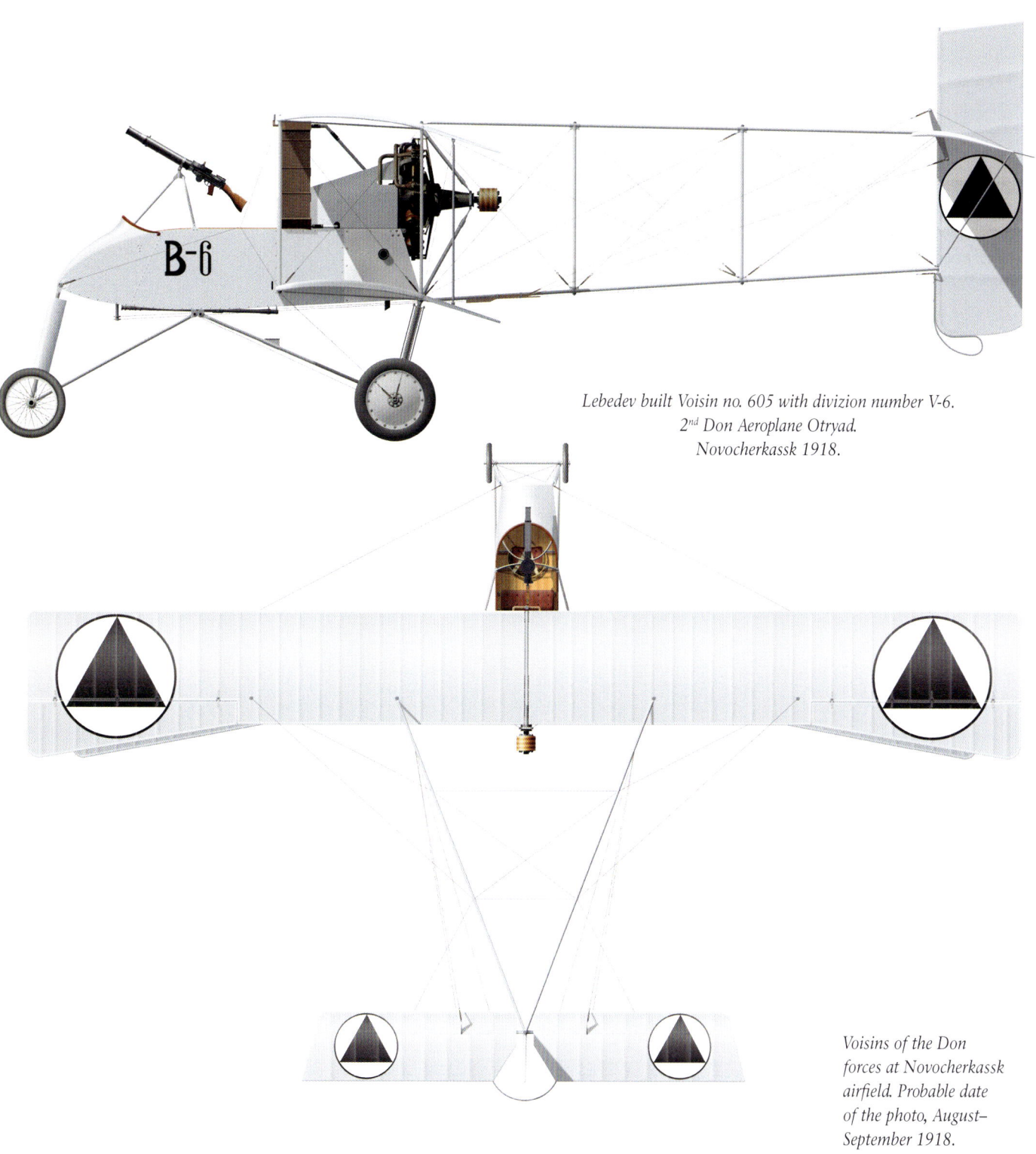

*Lebedev built Voisin no. 605 with divizion number V-6.
2nd Don Aeroplane Otryad.
Novocherkassk 1918.*

Voisins of the Don forces at Novocherkassk airfield. Probable date of the photo, August–September 1918.

21

French production Voisin no. 1280 with divizion no. 3. Don Aviation Park. Novocherkassk, 1918.

For easier recording, the aeroplanes started to be allocated numbers within the division: these were ordinal numbers for each type.

> **Orders for the Don Aeroplane Divizion No. 67**
>
> 11 December 1918 Novocherkassk
>
> §3.
> ON THE TECHNICAL PART
>
> I submit, in all Otryads, to apply now the division numbers of the aeroplanes on both sides of the fuselages (or on the nacelles) of the aeroplanes.
>
> I request that you do not maintain an Otryad numbering nor place it on aeroplanes to avoid confusion.
>
> The Divizion numbering will be maintained separately for each aircraft type.
>
> When releasing aeroplanes from the workshops of the base or the Park, they must be marked with an appropriate divizion number.
>
> §4.
>
> I announce the register of the Divizion aeroplanes with the indication of factory and Divizion numbers:
>
> | Type | Divizion no. | Factory no. | Notes |
> |---|---|---|---|
> | Morane Monocoque | 1 | 748 | Divizion HQ |
> | Nieuport-XXIII | 1 | 3707 | 1st Don Aeroplane Otryad |
> | Nieuport-XXIII | 2 | 3213 | 1st Don Aeroplane Otryad |
> | Nieuport-XXIII | 3 | 2992 | 1st Don Aeroplane Otryad |
> | Nieuport-XXIII | 4 | 3355 | 2nd Don Aeroplane Otryad |
> | Nieuport-XXIII | 5 | 3595 | 2nd Don Aeroplane Otryad |
> | Nieuport-24 | 6 | 5422 | 9th Army Otryad |
> | Nieuport-XXIII | 7 | 3156 | 9th Army Otryad |
> | Nieuport-XXIII | 8 | 5059 | 9th Army Otryad |
> | Nieuport-XXIII | 9 | w/o no. | 9th Army Otryad |
> | Sopwith | 1 | w/o no. | 2nd Don Aeroplane Otryad |
> | Sopwith | 2 | 2358 | 9th Army Otryad |
> | Sopwith | 3 | w/o no. | 9th Army Otryad |
> | Sopwith | 4 | 1542 | overhaul at Taganrog |
> | Sopwith | 5 | w/o no. | overhaul at Taganrog |
> | Spad I.S. | 1 | 1472 | 2nd Don Aeroplane Otryad |
> | Spad I.S. | 2 | 1547 | 9th Army Otryad |
> | Farman-XXX | 1 | 1887 | 1st Don Aeroplane Otryad |
> | Farman-XXX | 2 | 1236 | 2nd Don Aeroplane Otryad |
> | Voisin | 2 | 421 | at the Park |
> | Voisin | 3 | 1280 | at the Park |
> | Voisin | 4 | 630 | 1st Don Aeroplane Otryad |
> | Voisin | 5 | 698 | 2nd Don Aeroplane Otryad |
> | Voisin | 6 | 605 | 2nd Don Aeroplane Otryad |
> | Voisin | 7 | 643 | 2nd Don Aeroplane Otryad |
> | Voisin | 8 | w/o no. | assembled from parts, 2nd Don Aeroplane Otryad |
> | Voisin | 9 | 628 | 1st Don Aer |
>
> *Divizion Commander, military pilot podpolkovnik Baranov**
>
> * *RGVA. F. 39457. Op. 1. D. 399. L. 63.*

In fact, the division numbers are not visible in many photos, obviously because of their small size.

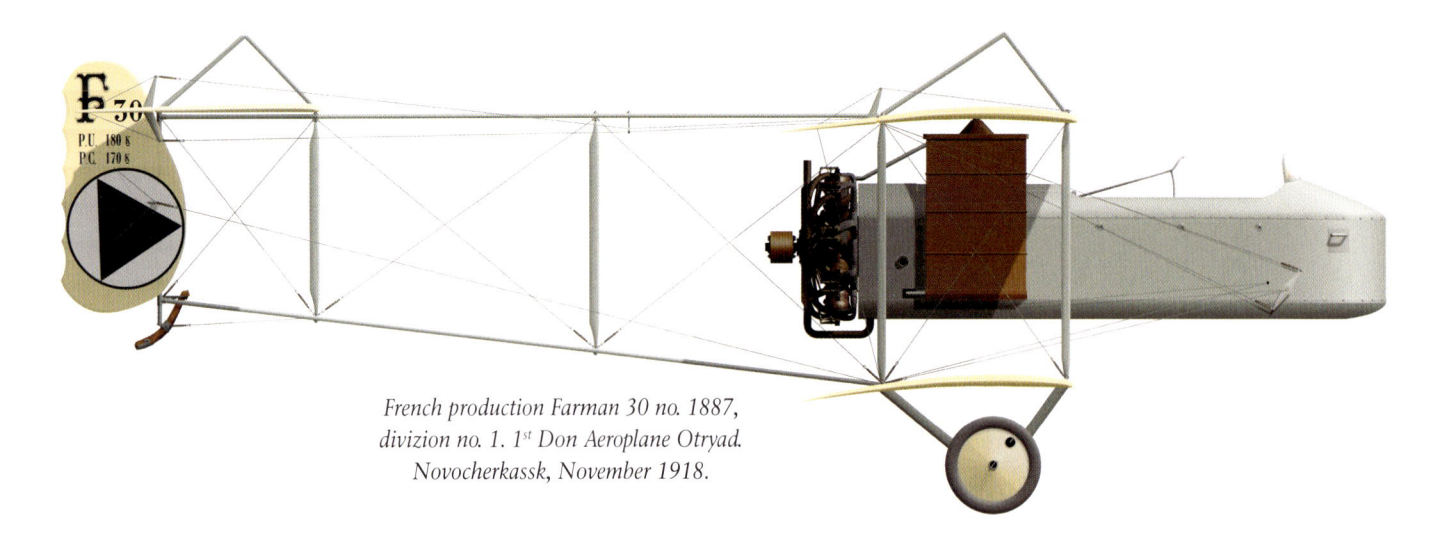

French production Farman 30 no. 1887, divizion no. 1. 1ˢᵗ Don Aeroplane Otryad. Novocherkassk, November 1918.

Inspection of the 1ˢᵗ Don Aeroplane Otryad during the visit of officers of the Anglo-French military mission of General Poole. The photo shows two of the five aeroplanes of the otryad: a Nieuport 23 and a Farman 30. Novocherkassk, 12/25 November 1918.

For example, the Morane Monococque that belonged to the Don Aeroplane Divizion HQ featured the old Russian national markings.

At the end of October 1918 the Don Aviation acquired a third otryad. At once six aeroplanes (two Sopwiths, three Nieuport 23s and a Nieuport 24*bis*) flew into the territory of the Almighty Don Host. The Red aviation suffered a serious loss, as the entire 9ᵗʰ Army Aviation Otryad defected: the otryad commander Snimshchikov, pilots Baranov, Dobrovol'skiy, Makarenko, Ostashevskiy and Khomich, observer Alad'in and quartermaster Khashkovskiy. Until the winter of 1918–1919 the otryad flew virtually no combat missions due to lack of petrol and spare parts. The personnel and materiel of the 9ᵗʰ Army Otryad was soon sent from the front to the rear, to Novocherkassk, where the pilots and aeroplanes were distributed among the newly formed otryads.

Several machines were delivered to the 3ʳᵈ Don Aeroplane Otryad, which started forming in the winter of 1918–1919. Surviving photos of the crashed Nieuport 23 which had earlier belonged to the 9ᵗʰ Army Aviation Otryad, show clearly the Don recognition markings, divizion number and emblem on both sides of the fuselage. The orders no. 348 did not specify on which parts of the aircraft the Don national markings should be applied. So, on this machine the black triangles on white discs were only at the bottom and top of the upper wing.

The artwork on both sides of the Nieuport is of interest. Perhaps this is the first case of caricatures drawn on an aeroplane during the Civil War period. The artist depicted *predrevvoyensovet* (Chairman of the Revolutionary Military Council) Trotsky in the form of a winged devil with pince-nez, greedily squeezing bags of food, a bottle and money. The Don Cossacks fiercely hated the Bolsheviks and depicted them in posters in the form of evil spirits. However, the 'propaganda' aeroplane did not last long and crashed during one of its sorties. This happened in April 1919, exactly at the time when aeroplanes of the Reds raided Novocherkassk.[12]

---

[12] For more details on these events see M. A. Khairulin's article "Fotografii s Grazhdanskoy… Nalëty aviatsii krasnykh na Novocherkassk, Rostov-na-Donu i stanitsu Veshenskaya v 1919 godu" ("Photographs from the Civil War… Raids of the Red aviation on Novocherkassk, Rostov-na-Donu and stanitsa Veshenskaya in 1919"), published in the "Donskiye kazaki v bor'be s bol'shevikami" ("Don Cossacks in combat against the Bolsheviks") almanac, No. 5/2011, pp. 119–131.

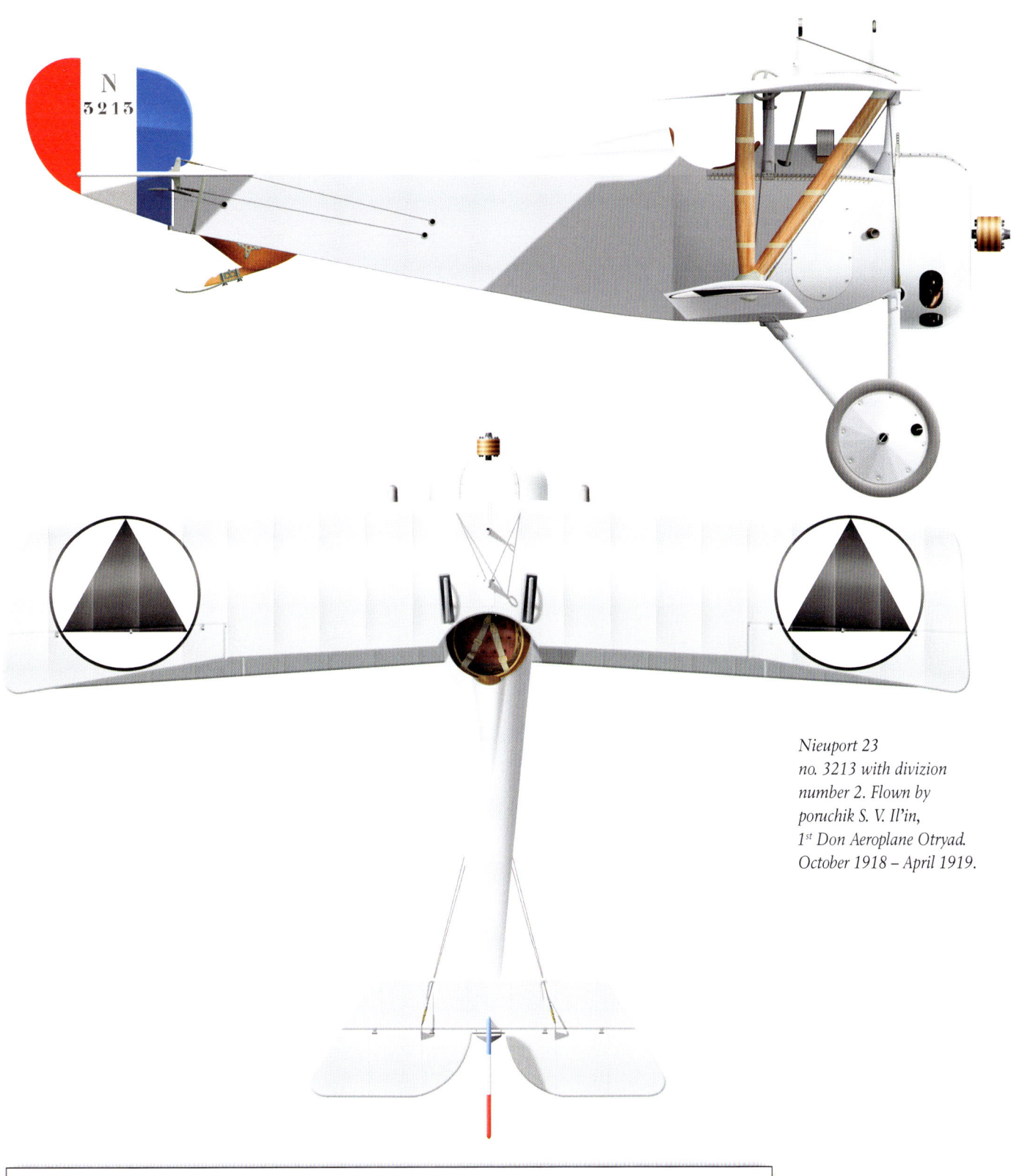

*Nieuport 23
no. 3213 with divizion
number 2. Flown by
poruchik S. V. Il'in,
1st Don Aeroplane Otryad.
October 1918 – April 1919.*

*Nieuport 23
fighter no. 3213
of the 1st Don Aeroplane
Otryad. Novocherkassk,
November 1918.*

Morane-Saulnier Monococque type VI with the factory no. 748 and divizion no. 1. Flown by military pilot poruchik G. M. Kamenev, Don Aeroplane Divizion HQ. Novocherkassk. March 1919.

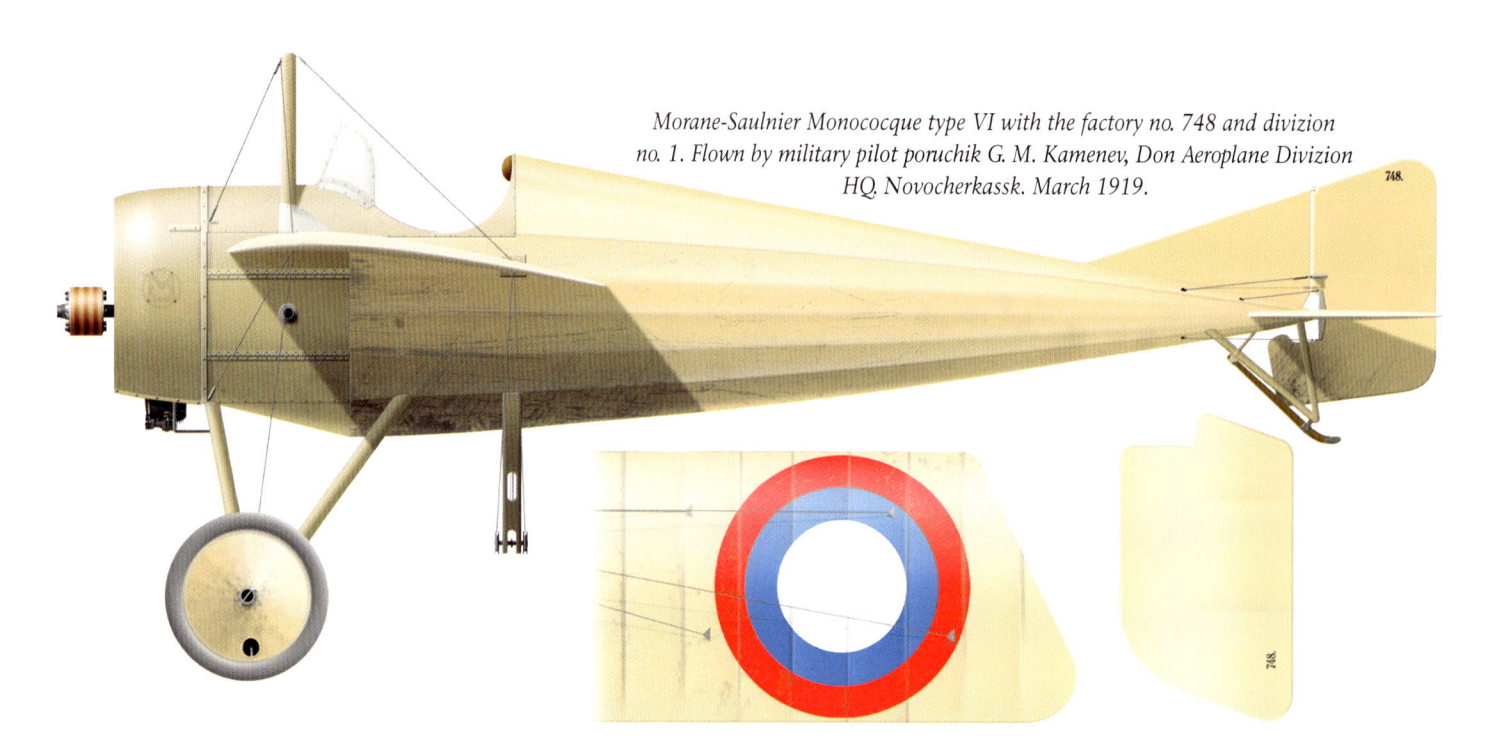

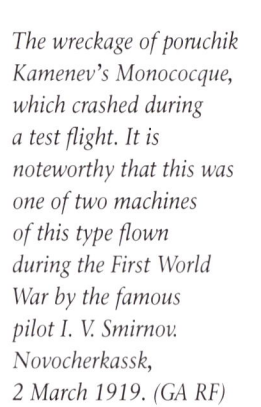

The wreckage of poruchik Kamenev's Monococque, which crashed during a test flight. It is noteworthy that this was one of two machines of this type flown during the First World War by the famous pilot I. V. Smirnov. Novocherkassk, 2 March 1919. (GA RF)

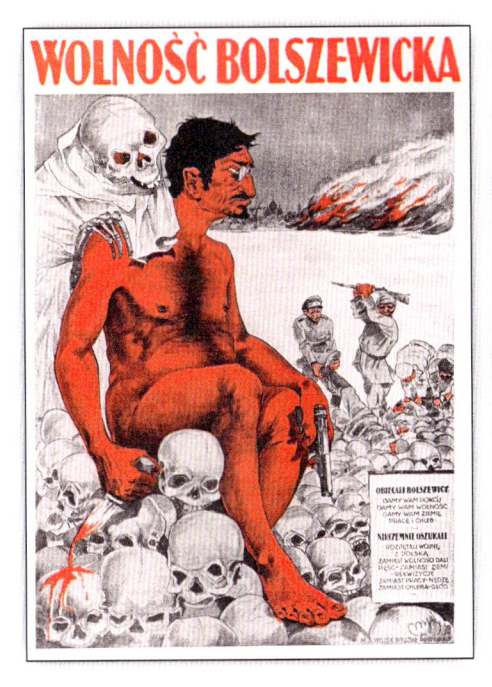

A Polish poster depicting Trotsky.   *A poster of the Don Department of Information. (GA RF)*

Lev Davidovich Trotsky (Bronstein). (From the collection of A. V. Ganin)

*Nieuport 23 serial no. N3156 divizion no. 7.
Flown by podporuchik V. I. Strzhizhevskiy. 3rd Don Aeroplane Otryad.
Novocherkassk, April 1919.
(The reconstruction of the emblem on the side
of the fuselage is copyright of T. A. Shtyk)*

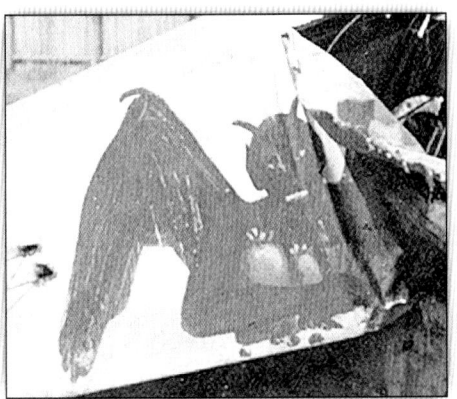

*The accident of Nieuport 23 serial no. N3156.
The aeroplane fell nose down from an altitude of 30 metres,
military pilot V. I. Strzhizhevskiy was unhurt.
April 1919. (GA RF)*

29

A Voisin of the 1st Don Aeroplane Divizion. The black triangle on the rudder is slightly off-set to the left and the divizion number on the nacelle cannot be seen. Novocherkassk, spring 1919.

A review of the Don Aviation in Novocherkassk during the arrival of the British military mission. Spring 1919. (GA RF)

Don aviation commanders: V. G. Baranov (in a papakha) and I. I. Strel'nikov in front of a Nieuport 21 with clearly visible markings on the wings. Novocherkassk, February–March 1919. (GA RF)

Information about the Don aviation would be incomplete without mentioning the aviation of the so-called Southern Army. The Southern Army was forming from September 1918 within the territory of the Don Host "*to liberate the Voronezh province from the Bolsheviks, and having its headquarters at Kantemirovka station*". Formation of engineering units took place at Chertkovo. The 1st Aviation Otryad was established from a pair of aeroplanes that had flown over from Ukraine. The plans of the Don HQ were much more extensive, as according to the orders no. 1192 issued on 11 October 1918 in Novocherkassk it was intended to form an aeroplane divizion of 3 otryads with 10 aeroplanes each as part of the Voronezh Corps of the Southern Army, and an aeroplane otryad of 10 aeroplanes as part of the Saratov Corps.[13]

These plans were not destined to come true. Only one aviation divizion with two otryads, of incomplete establishment, had been formed in the Southern Army by the spring of 1919.

The very first aeroplane of the 1st Aviation Otryad is of interest, as its history is very curious. On 20 July 1917 Brandenburg C.I, serial no. 64.67, of the Austrian *Flik 26* (26th Air Company) was shot down by *rotmistr* A. A. Kozakov, the commander of the 1st Combat Aviation Group and his assistant *pod"yesaul* I. A. Shangin. After a short joint attack the enemy descended in Russian-held territory near the village of Dolinyany, south of Khotin. The pilot, *Korporal* Trojan Varza, was killed in the air, and the wounded observer, *Leutnant* Franz Slavik managed to make an emergency landing. After landing the damaged aeroplane was captured. Veselovskiy himself was well acquainted with the Austrian machine, as in the second half of 1917 he flew Brandenburgs, nos. 270 and 64.67 in combat with the 8th Army Aviation Otryad. In March 1918 no. 64.67 was transferred, first to the 1st Ukrainian Aviation Otryad in Kiev, from where it was flown to the Don. In August 1918 *poruchik* Veselovskiy[14] flew the Brandenburg from Kiev to the Don along the route Kiev–Kharkiv–Kupyansk–Svatov–Chertkovo st. The distance of 1,100 versts took the pilot 8 hours 10 minutes to cover.

Aeroplanes of the 1st Aviation Otryad of the Southern Army. In front of the Brandenburg is a captured Sopwith in which N. Kuznetsov, a pilot of the 1st Aviation Otryad of the Smolensk Aviation Group made an emergency landing behind enemy lines. The machine retained the British national markings and the original number A8265. Chertkovo station, Winter 1918/1919. (GA RF)

13 RGVA. F. 40213. Op. 1. D. 1449. L. 149.
14 On 15 August 1918 znachkovyy Veselovskiy was the commander of the 2nd Artillery (Cannon) Aviation Otryad of the Chernigov Aviation Divizion in Kiev.

Hansa-Brandenburg C.I no. 64.67. Flown by commander of the 1st Aviation Otryad of the Southern Army poruchik V. S. Veselovskiy. The aeroplane displays recognition markings of the Don aviation. Chertkovo station, Winter 1918/1919. (GA RF)

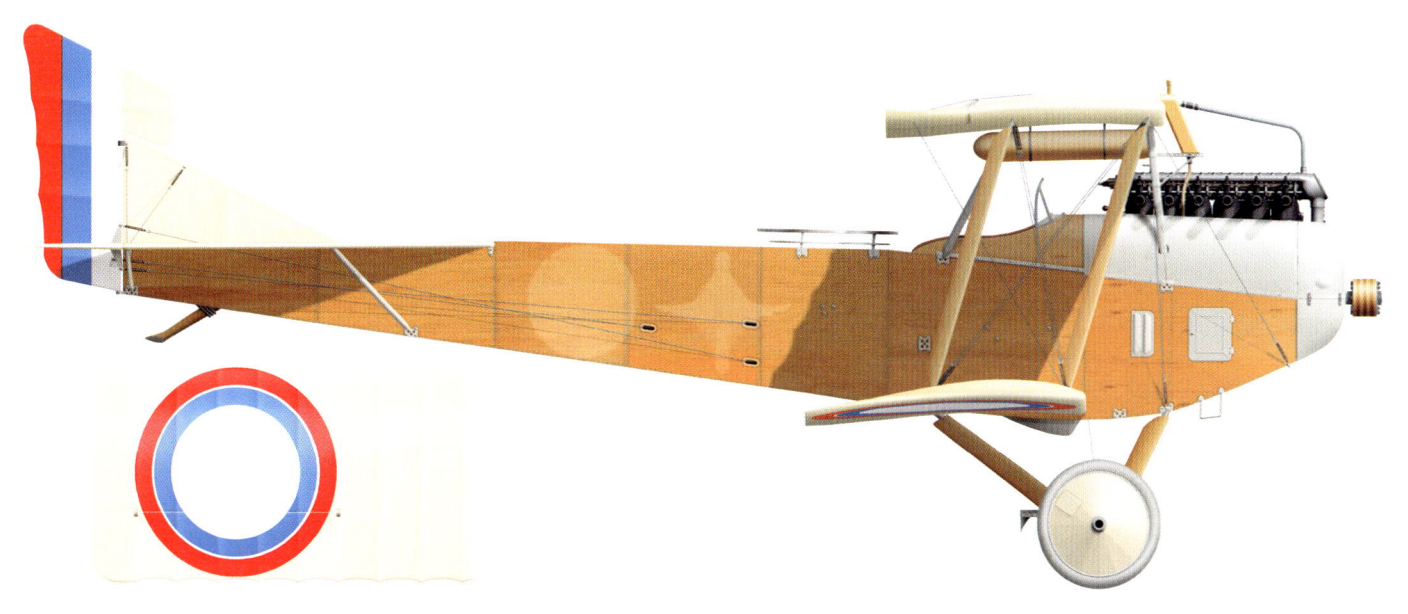

This is what the Brandenburg looked like during the flight to contact the Army of admiral Kolchak. The markings and emblem on the side had been washed off, and traditional three-colour roundels were applied on the wings. Summer 1919.

Military pilot kapitan Veselovskiy and observer poruchik Tikhanovich. Novocherkassk, June 1919. (GA RF)

33

Veselovskiy's flights for communication with the rebellious Cossacks of the Upper-Don district[15], as well as his long flight to the east for communication with the army of admiral Kolchak, are glorious chapters of his combat biography.

Information about the aeroplane even found its way into the memoirs of Gorbov, a former engine mechanic of the 'Brander', as it was affectionately called in the 1st Aviation Otryad of the Southern Army:

> "My duties as a mechanic were to supervise the engine of the commander's aeroplane. It was a captured Austrian machine. On its fuselage was its factory mark that had struck me forever: "Khanzabrandenburgishermiliterflugtseygautomobil'kraftverke"[16]. This aeroplane was old and well-worn; its full length was not just stained, but covered with castor oil."[17]

The Brandenburg displayed Don national markings on the sides and on the wings, and in June 1919 these were replaced by Russian roundels, evidently on the eve of the flight to Kolchak.

By 1 April 1919, as a result of the disbandment of the Southern and Astrakhan' Armies, their aviation divizions, all the time technically dependent on the Don aviation, became part of it, forming the 2nd Aeroplane Divizion at the Don Army, with its HQ, three aviation otryads and a mobile base. In total, six land-based aeroplane otryads were formed, and in the winter of 1918–1919, when the Don region was abandoned, the aviation section was reduced to three otryads. When remnants of the personnel and aeroplanes arrived in the Crimea, the Don aviation was finally disbanded in March 1920. The Don aviators formed the 2nd Don Aviation Otryad 'Host Ataman General Kaledin', which became part of the AFSR aviation, then the Russian Army, and fought successfully in the Crimea until November 1920.

Kuban' Cossack Host

A few words need to be said about the aviation of the Kuban' Cossack Host.

In December 1918 military pilot *polkovnik* V. M. Tkachëv[18] started forming the 1st Kuban' Aviation Otryad in Yekaterinodar, according to the instruction of the Head of the Engineers of the Kuban' Cossack Host and to the orders of the military staff.

They received their aeroplanes pretty quickly. In November 1918 the German-Austrian troops began to leave the territory of Ukraine. At the same time they left in Odessa more than a hundred Anasals, built to an order of the Austrian HQ. Thanks to the fact that the Allies supported general Denikin and his Volunteer Army, they 'generously' allowed them to collect the ownerless (and unwanted by the interventionists) aeronautical property in Odessa and its environs. Thus, the aviation of the White was considerably enriched with the aeroplanes manufactured by the A. A. Anatra factory.

Plant of aeroplanes
Artur Anatra
Firing field
City of Odessa

to the Aviation inspector
of the Odessa area of the Volunteer Army

"25" December 1918

Presently, a series of six "Anasal'" machines with engines of 150 power, with airscrews, radiators and machine gun turrets, are being built anew at the plant, which will be gradually completed within two weeks. Further construction of "Anasal's", taking into account that the factory has up to 50 semi-finished fuselages and a lot of skinless wings and tails, depends on the lack

---

15 For more details about the flights of the Don pilots see the article "Dorogiye ptitsy! Rabota lëtchikov Donskoy aviatsii vo vremya vosstaniya v Verkhne-Donskom okruge. Aprel' – iyun' 1919 goda" ("Dear birds! The work of the pilots of the Don Aviation during the uprising in the Upper Don district. April-June 1919") in the 3rd issue of the almanac.

16 The plate on the nose of the aeroplane had the inscription: Hansa-Brandenburgischer Militärflugzeug Automobil Kraftwerke.

17 Gorbov M. "Odisseya vol'noopredelyayushchegosya" („Odyssey of a volunteer"), "Voyenno-istoricheskiy arkhiv" magazine No. 9 (45)/2003 p. 42.

18 Vyacheslav Mikhaylovich Tkachëv, a Kuban' Cossack, a native of the Kelermesskaya stanitsa, Maykop county, Kuban' region.

of some special materials, such as: fabric, aircraft tar paper, etc. Salmson engines for these are available. Airscrews and radiators can be manufactured by the factory.

The factory, with the arrival of units of the Volunteer Army, immediately took steps to design and build radiators for the "Anasal's". The number should be sufficient both for the requisitioned "Anasal's" located at the plant, and those 20 "Anasal's" that were taken by your order from Odessa cargo station, as well as the "Anasal's", which can be built in the future at the factory.

Signed: by proxy A. A. Anatra – manager Ol'shanetskiy.

Listing of aeroplanes located at the Anatra plant in Odessa.

1. Anade. 47. Prepared for the installation of 110 hp Monosoupape, all in disassembled form, without the fittings for the airscrews, there are only 4 old engines.
2. Anade. 10. Prepared for the installation of 110 hp Clerget, no engines.
3. Farman XX. 35. Prepared for the installation of 80 hp Gnome, in disassembled form with fittings, 20 engines for these, no airscrews.
4. Morane G 14-metre. 6. Prepared for the installation of 80 hp Gnome, in disassembled form without fittings. Engines old.
5. Caudron. 6. Prepared for the installation of 80 hp Rhône, in disassembled form without fittings, there are old engines, no airscrews.

All these machines, to be brought into a completely finished condition, with engines and airscrews, will require the provision, by your orders, from the reserves of local aviation units, of engines and airscrews for these among them, which, according to this statement, do not have those, and the work on the installation of engines and necessary fittings can be made within a month from the date of receipt of your orders for the first 20 machines, provided that the engines are fully serviceable... In addition, there are 35* requisitioned Anasal' machines in dismantled condition, with engines and airscrews, 25 of them with dual control. All 35 without radiators. Four machines among this number with the installation of radiators on them, according to your proposal, are now assembled, inspected, adjusted, **repainted in national colours** and will be tested on the ground and in the air.

Note.
Completely serviceable machines as of 13/25 December 1918 from among these machines, the following machines earmarked for despatch to Yekaterinodar and to the Don with polkovnik Shimkevich:

1. Two Anades with Monosoupapes and airscrews.
2. Two Caudrons with Rhônes.
3. Two Moranes with Gnomes and airscrews.
4. Six Farman XXs with Gnomes.

Also for despatch to Kuban' at the orders of polkovnik Tkachëv, the following machines:

1. Two Anades with Monosoupapes and airscrews.
2. Two Moranes with Gnomes.
3. Four Farman XXs with Gnomes.

[...]**

* *The original tenor of the document.*
** *RGVA. F. 39540. Op. 1. D. 208. L. 3.*

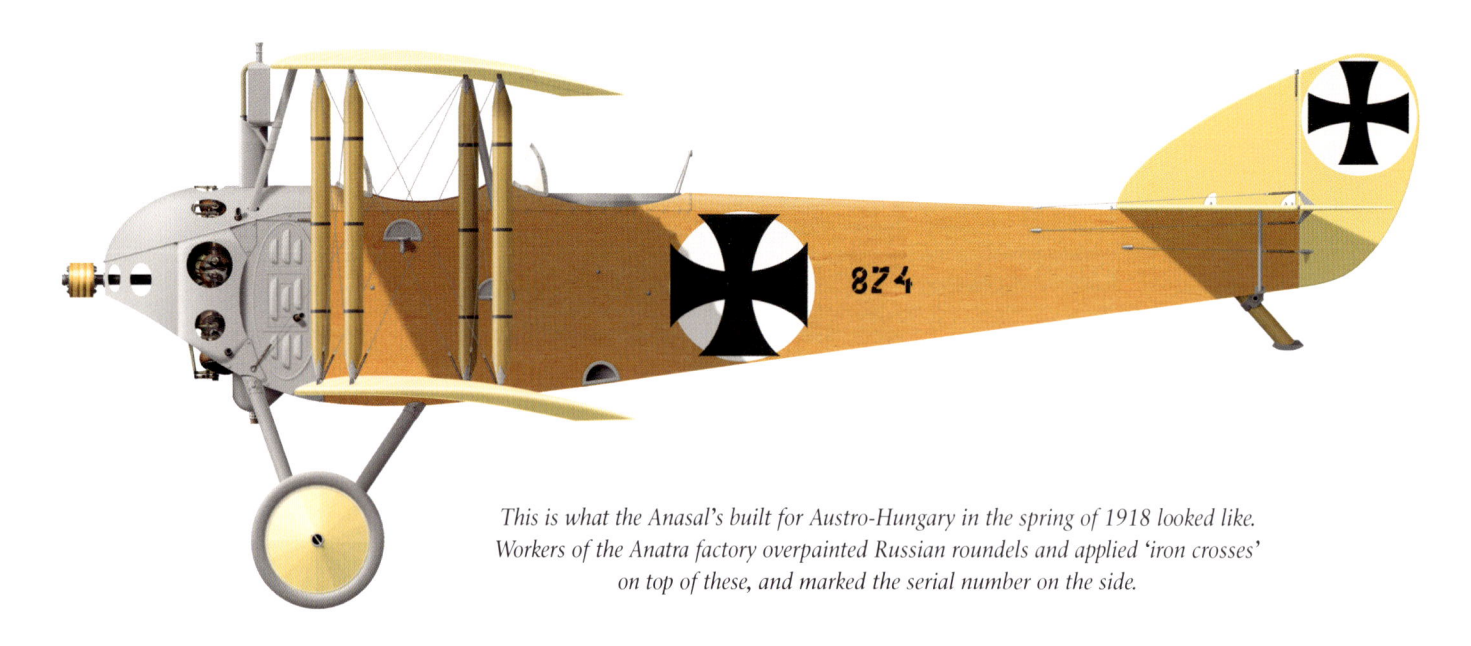

This is what the Anasal's built for Austro-Hungary in the spring of 1918 looked like. Workers of the Anatra factory overpainted Russian roundels and applied 'iron crosses' on top of these, and marked the serial number on the side.

By January 1919 the 3rd Aviation Divizion of the Volunteer Army began to form and, thanks to the Odessa reserves, three otryads were equipped to complete establishment. The Kuban' forces were not disregarded, either – eight or nine aeroplanes were despatched from Odessa by steam ship to Novorossiysk, from where they were delivered to Yekaterinodar.

As a result, by the beginning of February, the otryad's first machine, a Sikorskiy S-16 (brought by *yesaul* Lobov from Ukraine) was joined by a Nieuport 17 for Tkachëv, two Morane Parasols, Farman 20s, and five Anasal's.

In April, the first otryad moved to the Tsaritsyn Front, while the 2nd Kuban' Cossack Aviation Otryad began to be formed at Yekaterinodar. Together they formed the Kuban' Cossack Aviation Divizion, which successfully fought in the Caucasian Army until February 1920.

The Anasal' biplane with a 160 hp Salmson engine became the main aeroplane type of the Kuban' troops.

Anasal' with the Austrian number 010.160 and German crosses, photographed at the Yekaterinodar airfield in March 1919. This machine was flown in combat by military pilot yesaul M. G. Limanskiy from April to August 1919. (TsDAiK)

The unit did not yet have an otryad or 'Kuban" emblem, it contented itself only with the application of the three-colour roundels on its machines on top of the overpainted crosses.[19] The markings looked like target marks – the bright outlines of the cross showing through the Russian national markings. The original numbers on the sides were also left unchanged, and these appeared in the otryad reports.[20]

19   In 1915 the Austrians replaced their recognition markings (red-white bands) with German crosses. Later they changed the shape of crosses, following the German "fashion" with some delay.
20   The Kuban' Anasal's had Austrian serial nos. 010.135, 010.155, 010.157, 010.160, 010.167. In 1915 Austro-Hungary introduced a unified system of serial designations for aeroplanes of army aviation. Each aeroplane received a number in the "BCDE" format, where "BC" was the batch number, and "DE" was the number of the machine within the series. "B" denoted the manufacturer and "C" was that manufacturer's consecutive type number. "B" = 0 was allocated to foreign aeroplanes, while the remaining figures were assigned to Austrian firms. Machines from the A. A. Anatra factory had the prefix of 010, which meant "the tenth foreign"

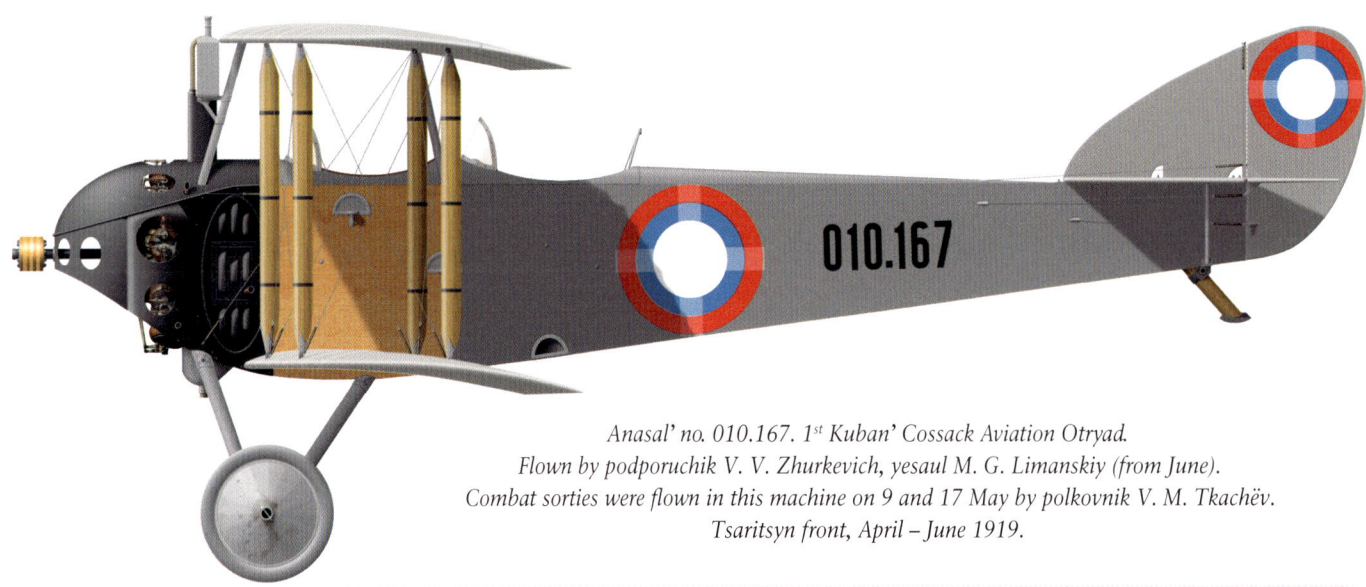

Anasal' no. 010.167. 1ˢᵗ Kuban' Cossack Aviation Otryad.
Flown by podporuchik V. V. Zhurkevich, yesaul M. G. Limanskiy (from June).
Combat sorties were flown in this machine on 9 and 17 May by polkovnik V. M. Tkachëv.
Tsaritsyn front, April – June 1919.

"Reconnaissance to Tsaritsyn" say the original captions. Roundels in Russian national colours on top of German crosses can be seen on the fuselage, rudder and wings of the Kuban' Anasal'. May–June 1919.

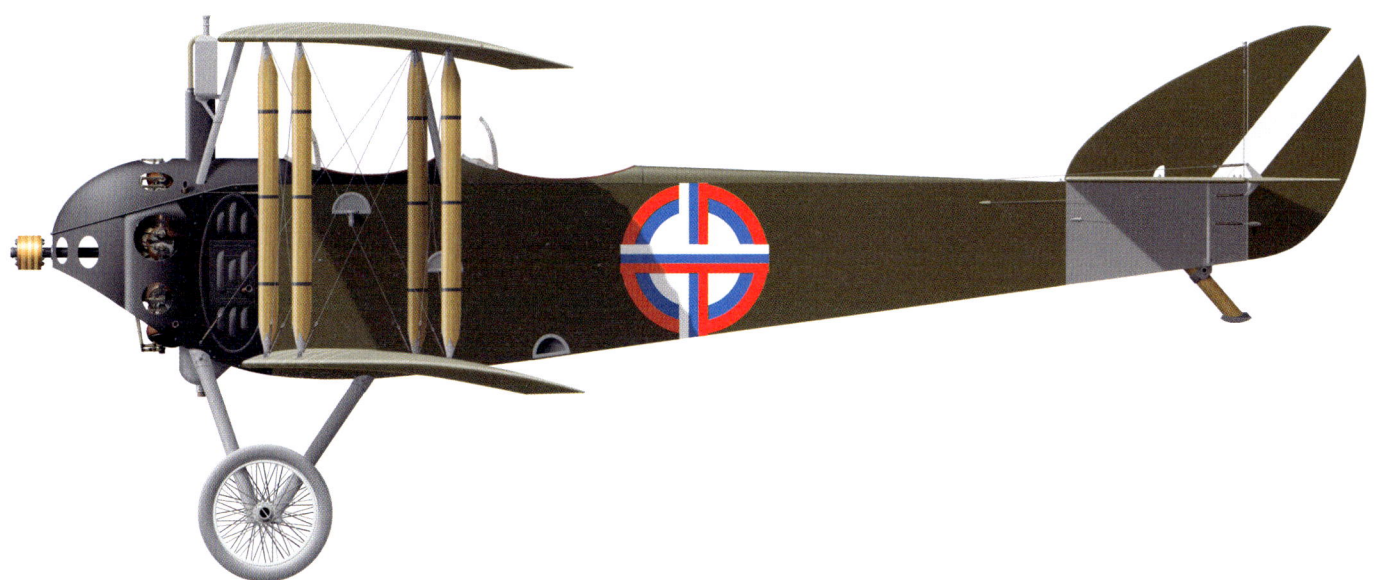

The aeroplanes at the airfield, left to right: Nieuport 17, Sopwith Camel, Sopwith 1½-Strutter, all with the Kuban' markings on the vertical tail, camouflaged in green and with roundels in Russian colours. In the foreground two R.E.8s with serial nos. E1128 and E1130, received in June for the 1st Don Aeroplane Otryad. A Nieuport fuselage with Russian roundels on the horizontal tail can be seen further behind, near the tent. A Kuban' Anasal' with a unique interpretation of the Russian national markings is visible on the right: the arms of the German cross, applied on top of the three-colour roundel, were repainted in Russian colours! Yekaterinodar, Summer 1919.
(TsDAiK)

In the summer, no later than July 1919, the Kuban' aviators started to use their own distinctive marking, a diagonal white strip on the vertical tail of the aeroplanes.

The first image of this marking was found in a photo of the Yekaterinodar airfield, where re-equipment of the Don and volunteer aviation otryads with British machines was in full swing.

So, the first aeroplanes to receive the otryad markings were the Nieuport 17, Camel and Sopwith 1½-Strutter.

Another series of unique photographs was included in an album of the 9th Red Army, thanks to which it has survived to the present day. It shows an intermediate airfield near the railroad leading to Novorossiysk, at Afipskaya or Krymskaya station. The photos were taken in the winter of 1919–1920, during the retreat of the White forces. They show Nieuports and Anasal's of the Kuban' units with the diagonal white stripe on the vertical tail. These were the last days for the Kuban' Aviation Divizion. In March 1920 the remaining personnel arrived in Crimea, at Feodosiya, without aeroplanes.

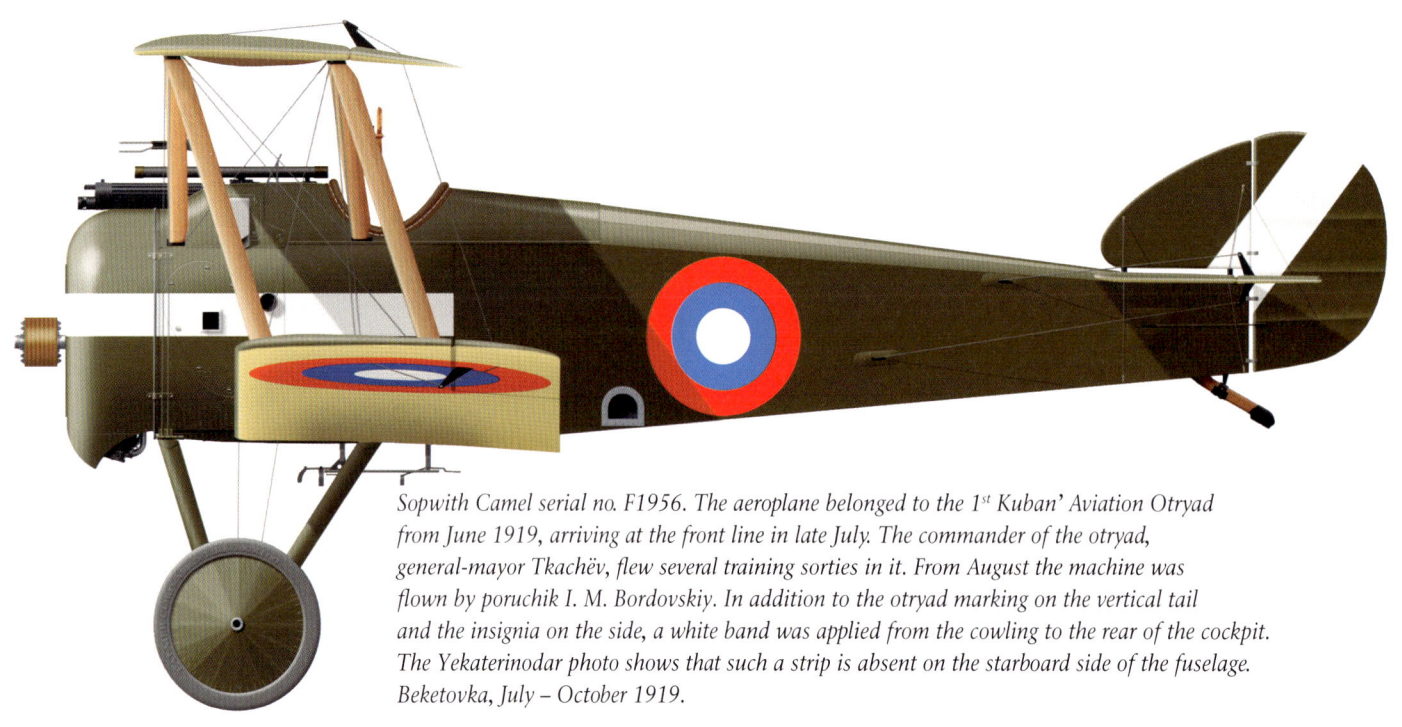

Sopwith Camel serial no. F1956. The aeroplane belonged to the 1st Kuban' Aviation Otryad from June 1919, arriving at the front line in late July. The commander of the otryad, general-mayor Tkachëv, flew several training sorties in it. From August the machine was flown by poruchik I. M. Bordovskiy. In addition to the otryad marking on the vertical tail and the insignia on the side, a white band was applied from the cowling to the rear of the cockpit. The Yekaterinodar photo shows that such a strip is absent on the starboard side of the fuselage. Beketovka, July – October 1919.

Captain S. Kincaid, 'B' Flight Commander in No. 47 Squadron, posing with Camel, serial no. F1956. The photo was taken in late September 1919, when the British Flight arrived at Beketovka, the base of the 1st Kuban' Aviation Otryad.
Together with No. 47 Squadron it was part of the so-called Caucasian Aviation Group.

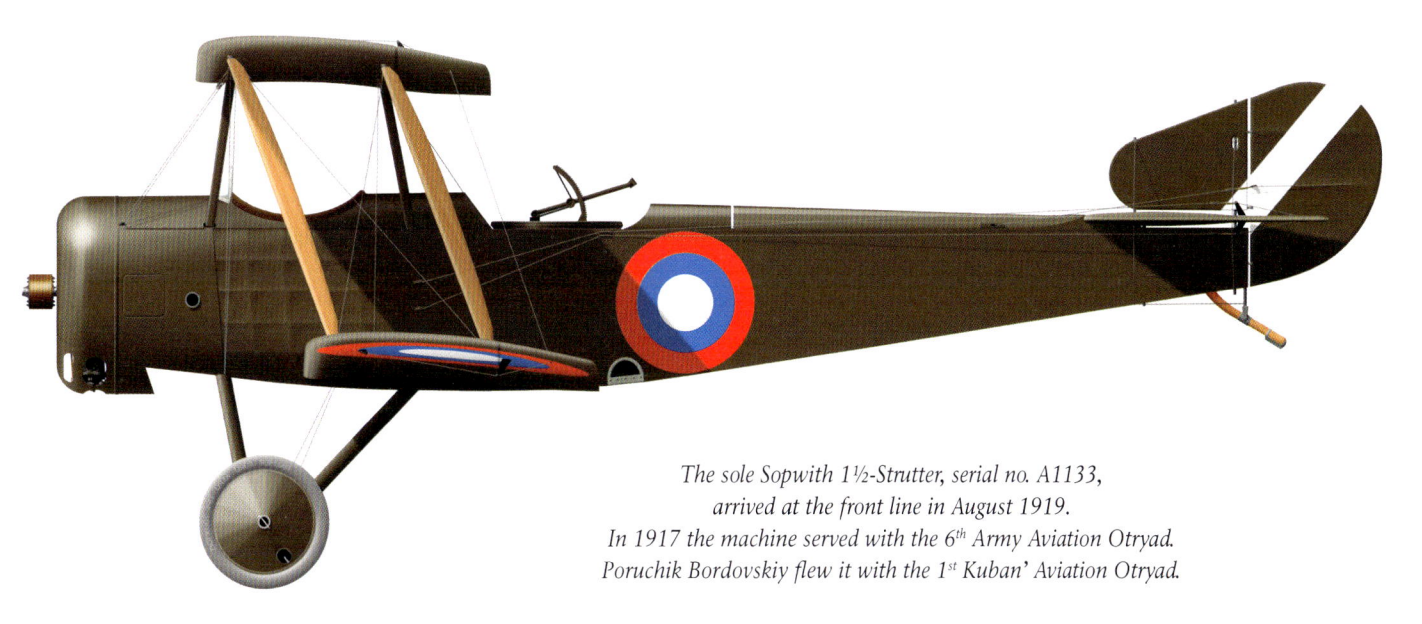

*The sole Sopwith 1½-Strutter, serial no. A1133,
arrived at the front line in August 1919.
In 1917 the machine served with the 6th Army Aviation Otryad.
Poruchik Bordovskiy flew it with the 1st Kuban' Aviation Otryad.*

An airfield of the Whites. Nieuports with the Kuban' markings can be seen in the foreground, a Voisin nacelle on the right, and British de Havillands in the background. The second photo depicts Kuban' Anasal's. Winter 1919/1920. (TsDAiK)

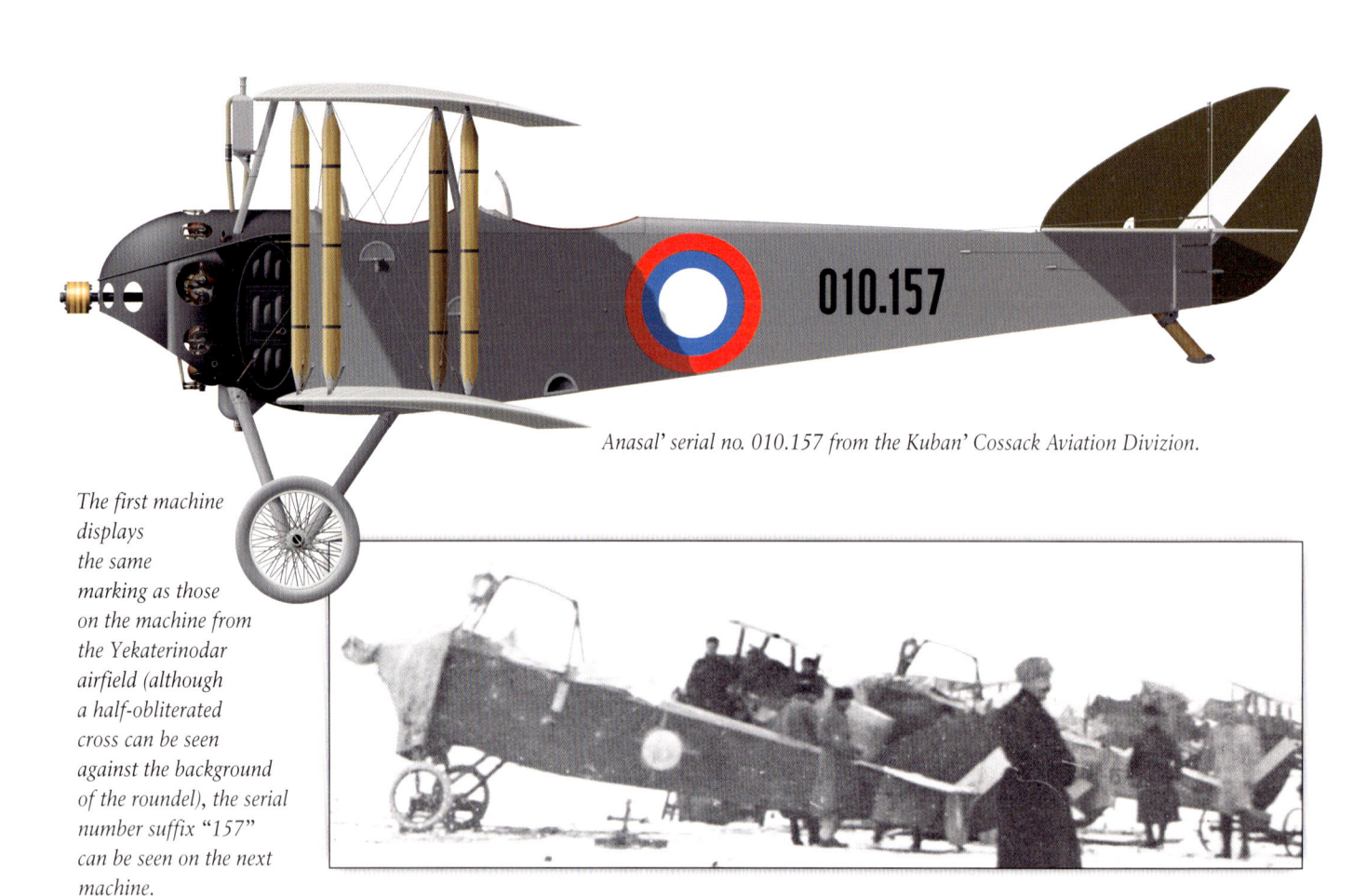

Anasal' serial no. 010.157 from the Kuban' Cossack Aviation Divizion.

The first machine displays the same marking as those on the machine from the Yekaterinodar airfield (although a half-obliterated cross can be seen against the background of the roundel), the serial number suffix "157" can be seen on the next machine.

A funny scene with a snow-covered Anasal'. The machine gun ammunition belt is the only sign of the former might of the winged machine, in its last days with the Kuban' aviation. Until not long before, brave aviators used it to cause fear among the cavalry of the Reds at Tsaritsyn.

Anatra built Nieuport 17s with three-colour roundels and Kuban' marking on the rudder.

Anatra built Nieuport 17s with three-colour roundels and Kuban' marking on the rudder. The marking features on the side of the first machine, but not on the second one. Roundels on the upper wings also differ. One of these machines was flown in combat in 1919 by the future head of the Russian Army aviation, general-mayor Tkachëv.

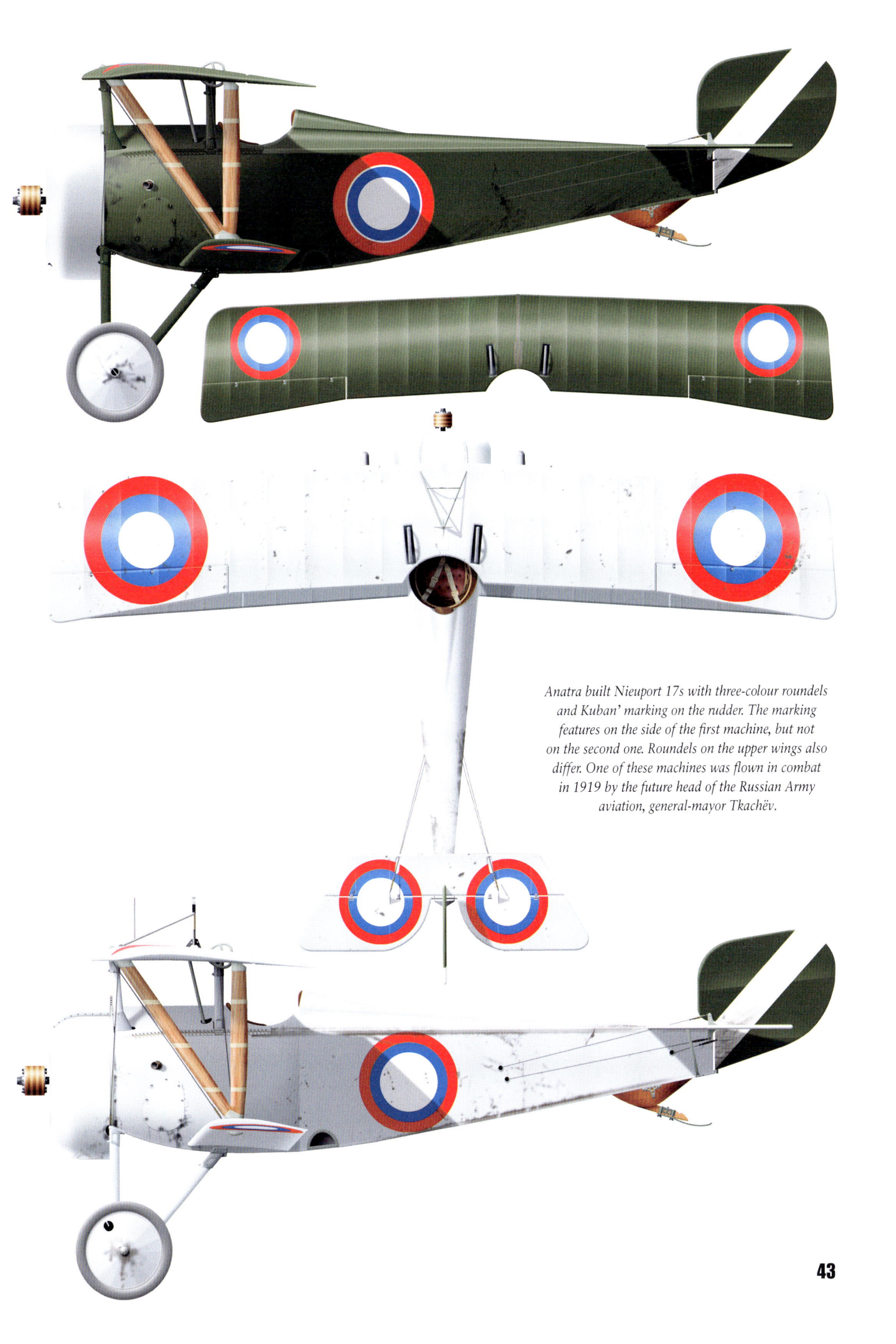

Forces of the Trans-Caspian Region

Information about the formation and further combat activities of the aviation of the Trans-Caspian Region Forces is extremely scarce. It is known that in February 1919 military pilot *poruchik* V. I. Yankevich was appointed commander of the Aviation Otryad of the Trans-Caspian Region Forces and arrived with it on 1 March at the disposal of the regional authorities. The otryad was included into the forces and throughout 1919 it constituted the aviation of the Trans-Caspian formation of the Whites. According to defectors' accounts the otryad had at least four aircraft, a Nieuport 21, a Farman and two Albatroses. In July Yankevich was replaced by *podporuchik* Morozov. Despite its small numbers, the otryad was active. It carried out reconnaissance, bombing and strafing of enemy troops. In late October it even fought an air combat. Morozov's fighter attacked a Farman 30 flown by a pilot of the 43rd Reconnaissance Aviation Otryad, led by Starodumov. According to the report of the Red pilot, he "*fired up to 30 bullets from a long distance, but then withdrew, without coming closer.*"

The marking of the aviation otryad was reconstructed according to a single photograph: the two-headed eagle from the period of the Provisional Government. The fighter was captured by Red troops at Kazandzhik station in early December 1919.

Duks-built Nieuport 21 no. 1948. This machine was flown in combat by the commander of the Aviation Otryad of the Trans-Caspian Region Forces, podporuchik S.I. Morozov. Kazandzhik station, December 1919.

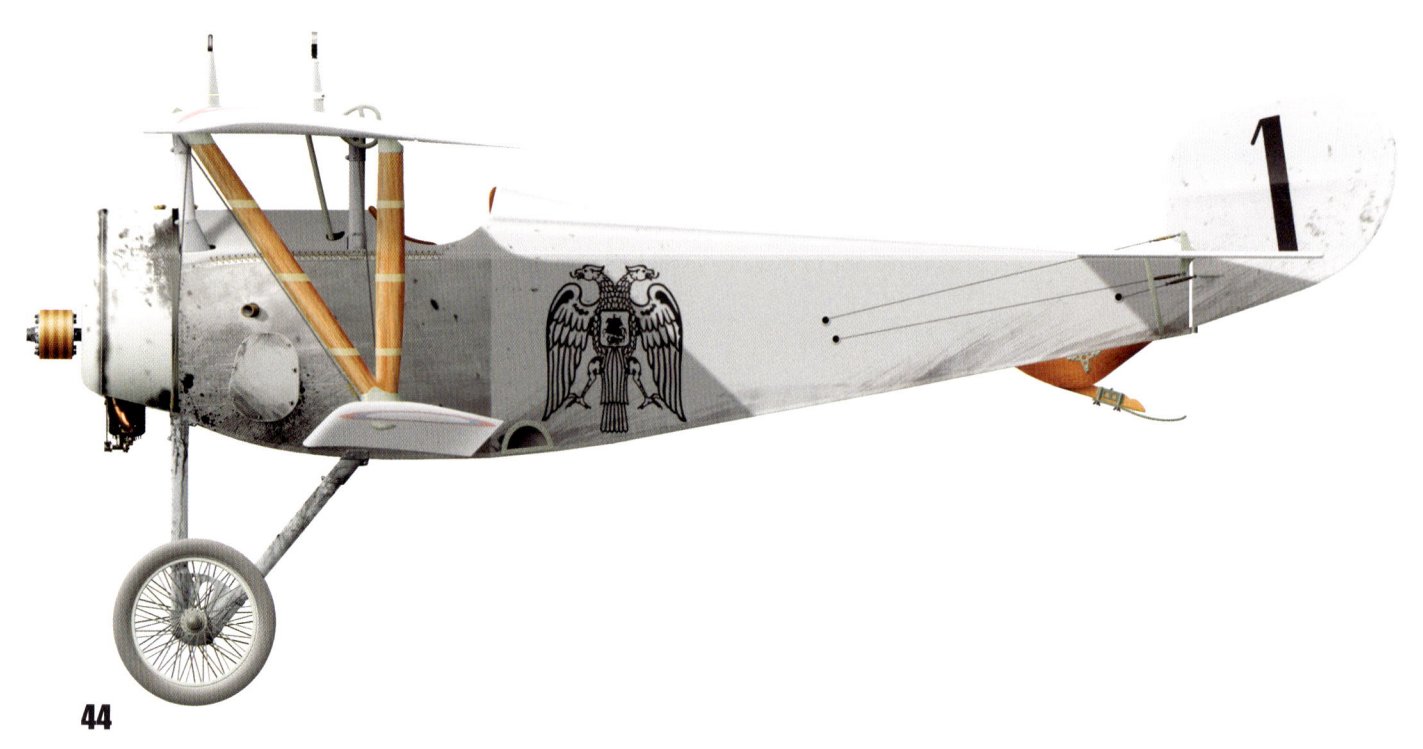

Aviation of the Russian Army

At the end of 1919, the general withdrawal of General Denikin's Volunteer Army to the Crimea was decided. At the time the 1st Aviation Park was in the Crimea (at Simferopol), the Military Aviation School was located at Kacha (near Sebastopol), but there were no combat aviation units there yet. With great difficulty, the 1st, 5th, and then the 3rd and 8th Aviation Otryads broke through to the Crimea, and they managed to bring aeroplanes with them. Remnants of other otryads arrived without their machines or support units. While the AFSR had 19 combat aviation otryads in the autumn of 1919, the Russian Army of *general-leytenant* P. N. Vrangel' in the Crimea had only seven aviation otryads of incomplete establishment by November 1920.

In January 1920, when hostilities began on the Crimean front, the situation was so critical that the whole burden of the work fell on the old training aeroplanes that arrived from Kacha to Dzhankoy.

In mid-February, at Dzhankoy, the first arriving aviation otryads (the 5th and 8th) formed the "Combat Aviation Group in the Crimea" under *polkovnik* M. Ye. Gartman. On 10 April *podpolkovnik* K. N. Antonov became the Commander of the Crimean group, which was also joined by the 4th Aviation Otryad.

And on April 14 the well-known pilot, *general-mayor* V. M. Tkachëv, took command of the White aviation in the Crimea. During 1914–1917 he was the commander of the 20th Corps' Aviation Otryad, the aviation inspector of the South-Western Front, then the Head of the Field HQ of aviation and aeronautics at the Staff of the Supreme Commander-in-Chief. During the war he had shown himself as a great pilot, a major organiser and skilful leader of aviation units of the Russian army. His competent leadership and his gift as an aviation commander played a huge role in restoring the decadent White aviation in the south of Russia. Due to the shortage of aeroplanes, the personnel underwent considerable selection. Much attention was paid to tactical training. Three otryads (the 1st, 4th and 5th) were equipped with the best machines at that time, the British two-seat de Havilland bombers (DH.9 and DH.9a). These machines were fitted with the 230 hp Siddeley Puma and 400 hp Liberty engines, respectively. The de Havilland DH.9s were armed, as standard, with two machine guns (a synchronised Vickers firing through the propeller disc and a Lewis on a rotating mount in the observer's cockpit) and could carry up to 210 kg of bombs. The fuel capacity allowed the machine to stay airborne for up to 5 hours. Despite the good characteristics, all the machines were old, having earlier served with the British. In the Crimea and Northern Tavriya the small aviation of the White forces, thanks to Tkachëv's skilful leadership, became a formidable opponent for the Red forces.

To make effective use of the limited aviation resources, it had long been necessary to introduce recognition markings to the otryads within the group, as well as for the aeroplanes of commanders and ordinary pilots.

In the memo of a pilot-observer of the 1st Aviation Otryad 'general Alekseyev', made in the spring of 1920, such plans were mentioned and variants of insignia, distinctive markings and numbers for the aeroplanes were suggested. The author of the memo, no doubt, based it on already existing examples. We quote the unique document almost completely.

"…Recognition markings and numbers on aeroplanes are divided into 3 categories:

I – markings for the aviation itself

II – markings for the [ground] troops

III – common markings.

I. It is necessary to have an otryad marking for two reasons:
First, each rank of the otryad will always try not to disgrace its insignia; second, with large formation flights, the leader can easily control the activity of each otryad.
Developing this idea further, we will see that it is necessary to have individual markings on machines in each otryad, the most convenient way is to have **Arabic numeral numbers**. In addition, for technical reporting, a factory number is required, which is required only on the ground, and therefore it may be applied just once in a certain place. Four-digit numbers in the size as applied at the park, begin to merge from a distance of 150-170 steps, and it is already impossible to distinguish such digits as 3 and 5. Their location on the machine is not very successful, especially the numbers on the rudder, with a presence of these on the sides of the fuselage; the location on the top surface of the bottom plane is incomprehensible.
If the numbers are of technical importance, then why is it needed to apply such digit sizes and why on these parts of the machine?

II. For the infantry, which the machine is supposed to support or with which it wants to communicate, it is best to combine a pennant on the rudder and on the struts, or a painted marking on the lower plane, between the fuselage and the plane in its entire width. For example, one of the machines of our otryad has the letter A applied with black paint on white background, no less noticeable than the English recognition marking.

III. To distinguish own aeroplanes from the enemy in the air, distinctive markings are usually applied at the tips of the upper and lower planes, on the sides of the fuselage and on the rudder. The most successful in this case are the markings of the German aviation, but we, of course, need to retain the **roundels of our national colours**.

First, because it is more national, and, second, the troops are already accustomed. The rudder is the most notable part and therefore it should be left common for our aviation, common for the entire aviation and clearly different from the aviation of the enemy. It is best, again, to paint **horizontal stripes of national colours**.

Among other things, the infantry identifies best according to the rudder. It has been observed: enemy machines had **black tail**, as the 8th Otryad; as regards the machine of the [Krym Combat Avation] Group HQ [podpolkovnik K. N. Antonov] with a **white German cross**, our troops said that this was "a German". […]

Group flight

The best way to identify a machine in the air, in addition to the otryad marking, is to give each machine an individual number within the otryad, written with Arabic numerals, on the sides of the fuselage, near the observer's cockpit, and in the middle of the upper plane. For recognition by our troops, it is best to paint the rudders with national colours."*

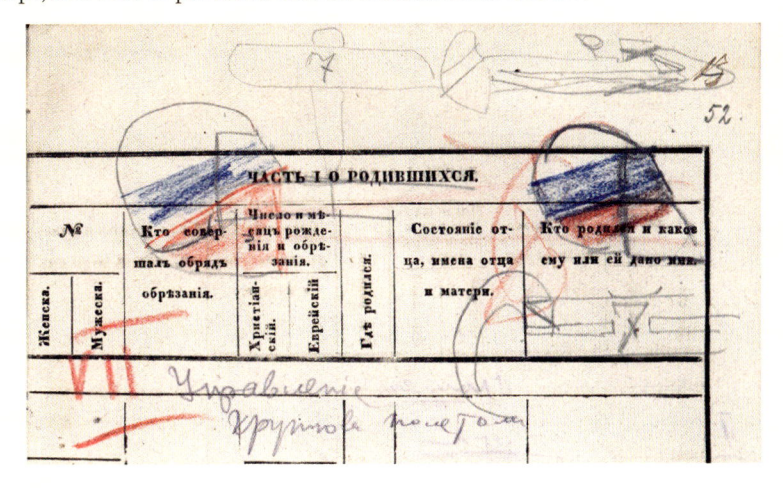

RGVA. F. 39527. Op. 1. D. 9. L. 8–10, 21.

Serial numbers (British as standard) remained in place, on the rear fuselage or on the rudder. And after a repair in a park only the digits of the serial number were left. Park or school[21] markings and numbers were applied on the sides of the fuselage or nacelle of the aeroplane, as well as on the rudder in some cases.

Let us consider the recognition markings that Vrangel''s aeroplanes had in 1920. They can be generally divided into three categories: 'old' three-colour roundels in Russian colours, British (or French) three-colour markings, and 'new' three-colour roundels of the Crimean period. The latter national markings will be discussed further in this chapter.

The first type of recognition markings remained on the machines since the First World War, or they were applied during an overhaul in a park or otryad.

Several sources confirm the recognition markings (three-colour roundels) of the Crimean period.

Journal of the Red Flyers

There, behind an impenetrable wall, far away, far to the north, in an alien, but native Moscow, a new magazine devoted to aviation and aeronautics was published: "Vestnik Vozdushnogo Flota" ("Journal of the Air Force").

This little book, its cover decorated with a propeller, leads to many heavy thoughts. This book – theirs, those who so recently flew with us, thought as we did, and shared with us all the hardships and adversities, giving their forces to the service of the Motherland.

But we have parted. They changed the Motherland, and we flew away from them. They are red pilots, we are Russians. Their sign – "R.S.F.S.R.". On their wings – a red star.

Our slogan, our sign, our goal – all for the suffering Motherland. On our wings – a **three-colour flag**.

And so – we follow separate ways.

But if any of them, those who are now serving the Internationale, comes to us and says that he sincerely repents of his error – we will not jostle him away. In the ranks of the Russian army there will always be a place for anyone who wants to redeem their grave sin before the Motherland.

*Nik. Shilov**

Zhurnal "Nasha stikhiya" No. 1 / August 1920, Simferopol', pp. 24–25.

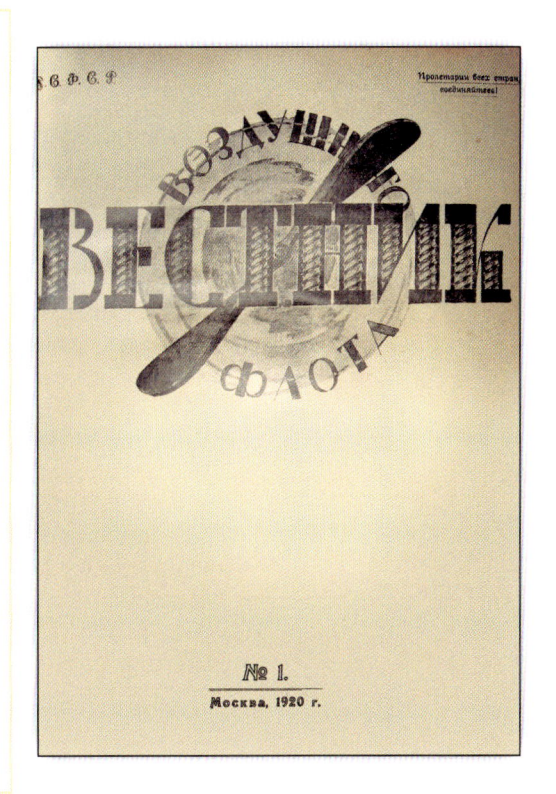

---

21 The aeroplanes for the front were repaired both at Kacha, and in the workshops of the Military Aviation School.

Let us quote an excerpt from the story of a combat sortie of a crew from the 48th Reconnaissance Aviation Otryad (pilot Malyarenko and observer Fradkin). They flew from Sofiyevka to bomb Melitopol', and spotted an enemy airfield along the way. That day, 19 June according to the old style, there were three aeroplanes of the 8th Aviation Otryad of the Russian Army at the airfield near the Fëdorovka station: an Anasal', a Nieuport and an LVG.

> *…The July morning broke out.*
> *Our Sopwith, loaded with bombs, bursts out of the hands holding it, rushes along the dewy grass and, smoothly breaking away from the ground, with all the power of a well-working engine takes us to a dangerous and high distance.*
> *We pass the front line. We are already above those who are afraid of us and to whom the crimson stars of our wings once again remind of the unavoidable and imminent death. An armoured train crawls to a bridge. In the very middle of it, two lights flashed one after another. Two more bursts catch up with us, and the train is far behind.*
> *Under us, shining with water and sands, the Dnieper.*
> *Soon it goes right, to the west, lazily curving, and we rush to our target, far to the south. We pass the stations one by one, and ahead, in the fog of the starting day, I can see a crossing of the railways. This is the Fëdorovka station. Here is the nest of the white ravens. Near a road, hugging each other, three aeroplanes stand there,* **sparkling with the varnish of the wings and the three-colour roundel on them.** *I involuntarily look at the machine gun, but Fëdorovka is already behind, and the white aeroplanes, still clinging to each other,* **look** *at our red stars through the eyes of their three-colour roundels. Pilot Malyarenko turns to me and shows something ahead. I nod my head: I can see, Melitopol'. I look back two more times, and still three aeroplanes doze at the station.*
> *The tension of waiting passes, and below us is a town of irregular streets and green spots of gardens. We go along the highway out to the station. Long snakes of echelons, smoking locomotives, crowds of people, horses and carts of the station and warehouses.*
> *We go against the wind on a smooth semicircle of the depot.*
> *I quickly tear off the fuse and throw a pood bomb down. A few seconds pass, and a column of smoke rises at the depot among the thick of the railway cars, and everything alive at the station flies in all directions in an indescribable panic. We go again, and two more bombs complete the effect. We are circling the station. Malyarenko turns back to me, sends an air kiss and, having reduced the throttle, trying to overcome the noise of the engine, shouts something. I cannot hear, but I understand that the words are funny. And there is something to be merry about. Behind the back of the three aeroplanes, probably more combat-worthy types than our Sopwith, we have so gloriously amused ourselves deep behind enemy lines.*[22]

Information about the distinctive markings can also be found in the excellent work of a former pilot-observer of the 5th Aviation Otryad of the Russian Army, *podporuchik* S. N. Pokrovskiy:

> *The flight usually took place in groups of not more than 7 aeroplanes in a Vic formation. With a larger number of aeroplanes they split into sections. The commanders' machines and the machines of various otryads had clear recognition markings (bright colouring of the rudder and nose and a wide band around the fuselage). Control was performed using the simplest signals – flares.*[23]

Thus, it is well known that all aviation otryads of the Russian Army in 1920 had their markings.

We will try to analyse the extremely scattered information about otryad markings with almost complete absence of photographs from that period that could be used to make unambiguous interpretations.

Let us mention perhaps the most famous photo, with the original caption of the "5th Aviotryad" and Baron Vrangel', who receives a report from a military pilot. It has just captured aeroplanes with an otryad marking. Despite the quality of the picture, the British serial number can be read: D2942. In 1919 and until the spring of 1920 the machine had fought with No. 47 Squadron RAF ('C' Flight, pilot Captain Anderson), and was then transferred to the Russian Army aviation. The rudders of several machines are adorned with black and white rectangles almost in chequered order. The picture, captioned *"Commander-in-Chief general P. Vrangel' receives a report of pilots"* was placed on page 45 of the magazine "Nasha Stikhiya" ("Our Element"; no. 1 of August 1920), published in the Crimea. According to another version, the photo was taken on 23 July 1919, when Baron Vrangel' was visiting the airfield of the 5th Aviation Otryad near Svyatyy

---

[22] Fradkin A. "V boyakh Grazhdanskoy voyny. III. Pokhvala Vrangelya" ("In combats of the Civil War. III. Praise of Vrangel"), "Samolët" magazine No. 11 (13) / November 1924 p. 21.

[23] Pokrovskiy S. "Rabota beloy aviatsii v Krymu i Severnoy Tavrii v 1920 godu" ("Work of the White aviation in Crimea and Northern Tavria in 1920"), "Vestnik Vozdushnogo Flota" ("Journal of the Air Force"), Moscow, No. 13/1922 p. 12.

Krest in the Northern Caucasus.[24] This version seems less convincing, since the otryad was based at Petrovsk and Logan' at that time. It really received the machines from the British No. 221 Squadron, as already mentioned earlier. The 5th Aviation Otryad even had a de Havilland with a similar number, D2948.

This picture was repeatedly published with the caption "Vrangel' during a visit to the 5th Aviation Otryad, Crimea, 1920".

Now let us return to Matveyev's book, excerpts from which were already quoted in Chapter 4. In exile, the author communicated with former aviators of the White armies, and on the basis of those stories he wrote his work.[25] And, indeed, it refers to the 'chess board'.

> *Two months later, Ivan Ivanovich was going on leave and in the corridor of the railway car he crumbled in apology before a sister of mercy, whose kerchief got caught on his new white cross of St George. Then, throughout the trip, he was talking to a young sister, telling her about his monoplane, which, unfortunately, had to be abandoned, since he returned with 48 holes from the last sortie and crashed it when landing.*
> *He showed photographs.*
> *"What is that ace of diamonds painted on your aeroplane?"*
> *"My emblem."*
> *"You chose, I should say, a prisoner's emblem", the sister laughed.*
> *Ivan Ivanovich smiled, too.[...]*
> *The White Front...*
> *Tsaritsyn. To the south-west, at the Beketovka station – an airfield.*
> *Ivan Ivanovich is busy with his newly received English Sopwith. The airplane is like a new one, but everything needs to be inspected, checked. He himself, with a mechanic, does not miss any part, bolt, buckle. Lovingly nurses every nut.*
> *"Done!" declares the mechanic joyfully, having screwed the last washed spark plug into the engine.*
> *"No, my friend, not ready. We have to dress it up", and Ivan Ivanovich began to paint a **chessboard on the rudder**.[26]*

With the help of the comparison table, where all known data are collected, we will try to understand the otryad markings.

24   G. L. Sheremetevsky. "Memoirs of a Russian Aviator. The Recollections of Georgii Leonidovich Sheremetevsky.", "Cross & Cockade" International Journal, Vol. 36, No. 4. p. 240.

25   Without a doubt, the text is literary, based on stories of "old" pilots. A real man, military pilot Ivan Mikhaylovich Bordovskiy, was undoubtedly the prototype of the hero of the chapter "Arestant" ("Prisoner"), a passage of which is quoted here. In the First World War he had served with the 2nd Corps' Aviation Otryad of the 1st CAG. Ace of spades was the emblem of the otryad, in the text it is represented as a diamond ace. Bordovskiy was awarded the St George's Sabre, and his prototype wore the Order of St George (cross). From August 1919 he really fought at Tsaritsyn and flew the Sopwith 1½-Strutter and Camel in the 1st Kuban' Cossack Aviation Otryad. Kuban' markings on aeroplanes are described above. In the Crimea, Bordovskiy became the commander of the 1st Aviation Otryad 'general Alekseyev', where the "chess board" probably served as the otryad marking.

26   Matveyev A. P. "Razbityye kryl'ya. Ocherki iz zhizni russkikh lëtchikov" ("Spread Wings. Stories from the lives of Russian aviators") Berlin 1936. "Arestant" ("Prisoner"). p. 144–145.

	Interrogation report of the photogrammetrist Leonid Arkad'yevich Ovtsyn, who defected from Vrangel' armies, dated 3/16 October 1920* *RGVA. F. 30. Op. 1. D. 231. L. 44–48.*	**Telegram to the Field Headquarters of the 6th Army for the Head of the Southern Aviation Group from the Headquarters of the Air Fleet of the Southern Front, no. 421, dated 4 November 1920*** *RGVA. F. 245. Op. 3. D. 218. L. 26.*	**Orders no. 53/203 of the 1st Horse Army's Red Air Force. 20 October 1920*** *RGVA. F. 189. Op. 3. D. 961. L. 61.*
The name of the aviation unit	From April 1919 I was serving in the 1st Aviation Park of the Volunteer Army. On 29 July 1919 the 1st Aviation Park moved to the Anatra plant in Simferopol'. Head of the park – shtabs-kapitan Sokolov. … The park is engaged in overhaul of the de Havillands with the Puma and of other aeroplanes.	Information on Vrangel' aviation as of 8 October (25 September of the old style) 1920. On the sector of the 13th Army, the air group of polkovnik Antonov is working, composed of aviation otryads: 1st, 2nd, 3rd, 4th, 5th and 8th.	In view of the transfer of the 1st Horse Army to the Vrangel' Front, I announce the information on the Air Fleet of the enemy according to the data from agents and information received from our pilots.
1st Aviation Otryad ['general Alekseyev']	Identification markings: rudder painted in checkerboard pattern – square black, white and grey. Roundels three-colour. A white arrow on the fuselage. Aeroplanes have different colours. A total of four de Havillands.	Identification markings: rudder painted in white and black squares in checkerboard pattern. Arrow along the entire fuselage. Four de Havillands.	–
2nd Aviation Otryad ['Don Host Ataman General Kaledin']	Flies the Avro with the Rhône, a total of six aeroplanes. Identification markings: half red and half white band on the rudder.	Six Avro. Identification markings: rudder painted half black and half white.	Equipped with 10 Avro aeroplanes with 130 hp Clerget, machine guns in the cabin. Distinctive marking of the aeroplane: square stabilizer.

	Interrogation report of the photogrammetrist Leonid Arkad'yevich Ovtsyn, who defected from Vrangel' armies, dated 3/16 October 1920* *RGVA. F. 30. Op. 1. D. 231. L. 44–48.	Telegram to the Field Headquarters of the 6th Army for the Head of the Southern Aviation Group from the Headquarters of the Air Fleet of the Southern Front, no. 421, dated 4 November 1920* * RGVA. F. 245. Op. 3. D. 218. L. 26.	Orders no. 53/203 of the 1st Horse Army's Red Air Force. 20 October 1920* * RGVA. F. 189. Op. 3. D. 961. L. 61.
3rd Aviation Otryad	Marking on the rudder monarchic.	Two Nieuports, a Voisin and two Anasal's. Identification markings: on the rudder a three-colour flag.	–
4th Aviation Otryad ['polkovnik Kazakov']	The most militant otryad. Aeroplanes: de Havilland and a 5th one with Liberty at Akimovka. Identification markings: rudder white.	Five de Havillands. Identification markings: rudder white.	Distinctive marking – white rudder.
5th Aviation Otryad	Based at Akimovka (five de Havillands). Identification markings: black and white band.	Four de Havillands. Identification markings: rudder half white and half red.	It has seven de Havillands with the Puma and one with the Liberty. Distinctive marking of the aeroplane: on the rudder a red square with a black one inscribed in it and a white one in the latter.
6th Aviation Otryad	–	–	Forming with Nieuports in the Sebastopol Aviation School.

	Interrogation report of the photo-grammetrist Leonid Arkad'yevich Ovtsyn, who defected from Vrangel' armies, dated 3/16 October 1920* *RGVA. F. 30. Op. 1. D. 231. L. 44–48.*	**Telegram to the Field Headquarters of the 6th Army for the Head of the Southern Aviation Group from the Headquarters of the Air Fleet of the Southern Front, no. 421, dated 4 November 1920*** *RGVA. F. 245. Op. 3. D. 218. L. 26.*	**Orders no. 53/203 of the 1st Horse Army's Red Air Force. 20 October 1920*** *RGVA. F. 189. Op. 3. D. 961. L. 61.*
8th Aviation Otryad	Aeroplanes: Nieuport, Anasal', LVG, de Havilland. Identification markings: black rudder.	Aeroplanes: Nieuport, Anasal' and LVG. Identification markings: black rudder.	It has: two Sopwith Camels, an LVG and five de Havillands with the Puma. Distinctive marking: on a white rudder area large black question marks.
Crimean Combat Aviation Group	–	–	It includes the 4th, 5th and 8th otryads. The commander of the group, polkovnik Antonov and assistant polkovnik Kuteynikov fly two de Havillands. Their distinctive markings: a white cross on black rudder area.
Head of the Russian Army aviation (aviaglav) general-mayor V. M. Tkachëv	–	–	Head of the aviation general Tkachëv. He flies a Sopwith and a de Havilland. His markings: black parallel bands on the silver finish of the Sopwith and on the green one of the de Havilland. Black ailerons.

From the above it follows that markings of three otryads are known reliably: the 1st, 4th and 8th Aviation Otryads of the Russian Army.

First, the 'chessboard' is mentioned in Matveyev's book. Second, the table information also indicates the 'chessboard order' of white, black and even gray squares. The photo captioned "5th Aviation Otryad", where the 'chessboard' rudders can be seen, is confusing. We can assume, however, that the picture in fact shows aeroplanes of the 1st Aviation Otryad. The arrow on the fuselage is another confirmed marking of the 1st Aviation Otryad machines. Apart from the archival information, there is also a photo of poruchik Vnorovskiy's aeroplane, published in the Chapter 5 in the story about the 35th Reconnaissance Aviation Otryad.

The rudders of aeroplanes of the 8th Aviation Otryad were painted black, this is confirmed by several sources: the air observer of the 1st Aviation Otryad in his memo and the testimony of prisoners and defectors (in the above table).

The machines with white rudders were flown by the 4th Aviation Otryad, which is also mentioned in the comparison table. Readers have first learned about the existence of the otryad markings in Vrangel''s aviation from the book *"Protiv chërnogo barona"* ("Against the Black Baron") by Spatarel', which describes the air fighting between the Red and White aviation in the Crimea and North Tavriya in 1920. And the story there was about the "white rudders".[27]

> *Savin did not have time to finish speaking. From a violent explosion, the walls of the house trembled, glass rattled in the windows.*
> *I and the commissar jumped out into the street.*
> *Four black de Havillands with white tails flew towards the airfield. They were coming for a new attack.*
> *"That's from Shebalin's otryad", said Savin. "Remember, the telegram about the bombing of Kherson mentioned that the attacking aeroplanes had their rudders painted white..."*[28]

The markings of the HQ of the Crimean Aviation Group were referred to as the *"white German cross"* by army troops, and *"a white cross on a black rudder area"* in the intelligence information. It can be assumed that this marking depicted the Order of St George, 4th Class, its outline being similar to the well-known German (Teutonic) cross. Only the commander of the group, *podpolkovnik* Antonov and his assistant, *voyskovoy starshina* Kuteynikov had not been awarded the Order of St George. It may have been a cross with straight arms.

It is not quite clear what was the colour scheme of the rudders of the Avros of the 2nd Aviation Otryad, as accounts differ: *"half red and half white band"* or *"painted half black and half white"*. It is difficult to say what the bands were, vertical or horizontal, because no photos survive. The proposed reconstruction of the colour of the rudders is presented in the comparison table.

Things are also not simple with the 3rd Aviation Otryad. It is indicated that the rudders were painted in "monarchic" colours, or that they had "a three-colour flag" on them. What did Ovtsyn mean by "monarchic"? Black-yellow-white or white-blue-red? For the Bolsheviks all these combinations were the incarnation of 'tsarist' colours. As a rule, this term more often applied to the traditional 'besik': the white-blue-red flag.

Drawing from Boris Pavlov's book "Pervyye chetyrnadtsat' let" ("The First Fourteen Years") with the original caption "D. Katerlez. Aerodrom. Otvazhnyy Nieuport 5. Posledniy moment pered pod"yëmom. 21 iyunya" ("D. Caterlez. Aerodrome. Brave Nieuport no. 5. The last moment before the take-off. 21 June"). The author portrayed the Nieuport 23 of yesaul N. I. Prosvirin, a pilot of the 3rd Aviation Otryad of the Russian Army. That day the pilot flew to repel a Sopwith of the Reds, which raided Kerch'. Aeroplanes of the 3rd Aviation Otryad still displayed the school numbers. Iin addition to no. 5, there was also a Nieuport 23 no. 7.

A small drawing of aeroplanes of the 3rd Aviation Otryad was made from life by alekseyevets Aleksandr Sudoplatov. The artist represented three-colour roundels on the wings and rudders. A part of the volunteer chevron is even visible on the fuselage of the first machine!

---

27 When preparing his book, Spatarel' also used archive material: he saw the testimony of photogrammetrist Ovtsyn at the RGVA. Thanks to that testimony he learned about the white rudders, and about Shebalin, the former assistant commander of the 2nd CAG, which in 1917 included the otryad of the author of the book.
28 Spatarel' I. K. "Protiv chërnogo barona" ("Against the Black Baron"). M.: Voyenizdat. 1967 p. 120.

*"An enemy aircraft of the Nieuport type **with a three-colour stabiliser** was encountered over Kerch', which I have engaged in battle twice, after a successful burst from a machine gun the Nieuport entered a dive and crashed 5 versts south of Katerlez"*, wrote in his report Red military pilot Kaminskiy of the 35th Reconnaissance Aviation Otryad, who had flown reconnaissance over Kerch'[29]. This happened on 1/14 July, when podporuchik Shevchuk, a pilot of the 3rd Aviation Otryad, attacked the Sopwith of the Reds in his Nieuport 23 no. 7.

There is also a series of photographs taken in November or December 1920 in the building of the former A. A. Anatra factory in Simferopol', where the 1st Aviation Park of the Russian Army was located. The photos show several captured machines, de Havillands and Voisins.

A few words about the Crimean Voisins. Of the two available machines, a single one was assembled. Back in April 1920, the head of the aviation park reported that:

the park can assemble two more Voisins for the detachment. There is fabric for one of them (the Voisin broken by kornet Yeliseyev), and for the other one it can be stripped from the Parasol wings, available in a large number in the school.

A photo from the "Vestnik Vozdushnogo Flota": the Head of the Aviation of the 4th Army, Red military pilot N. V. Vasil'yev in the cockpit of a captured Ansaldo no. 13196. A striped Voisin tail section of the former 3rd Aviation Otryad of the Russian Army can be seen behind him.

In the hangar of the former 1st Aviation Park of the Russian Army. A Puma-engined de Havilland with a white rudder is in the foreground, with Voisin no. 52 behind it. Autumn 1920. (TsMVS)

---

29   RGVA. F. 192. Op. 3. D. 1352. L. 84.

The Voisin flown by yesaul A. A. Kovan'ko. The 3rd Aviation Otryad of the Russian Army. No. 52 on the rudder and on the nacelle an inscription of the 1st Aviation Park (Simferopol'): "No. 18. 1st Av. p. 19-19". Crimea. Summer 1920.

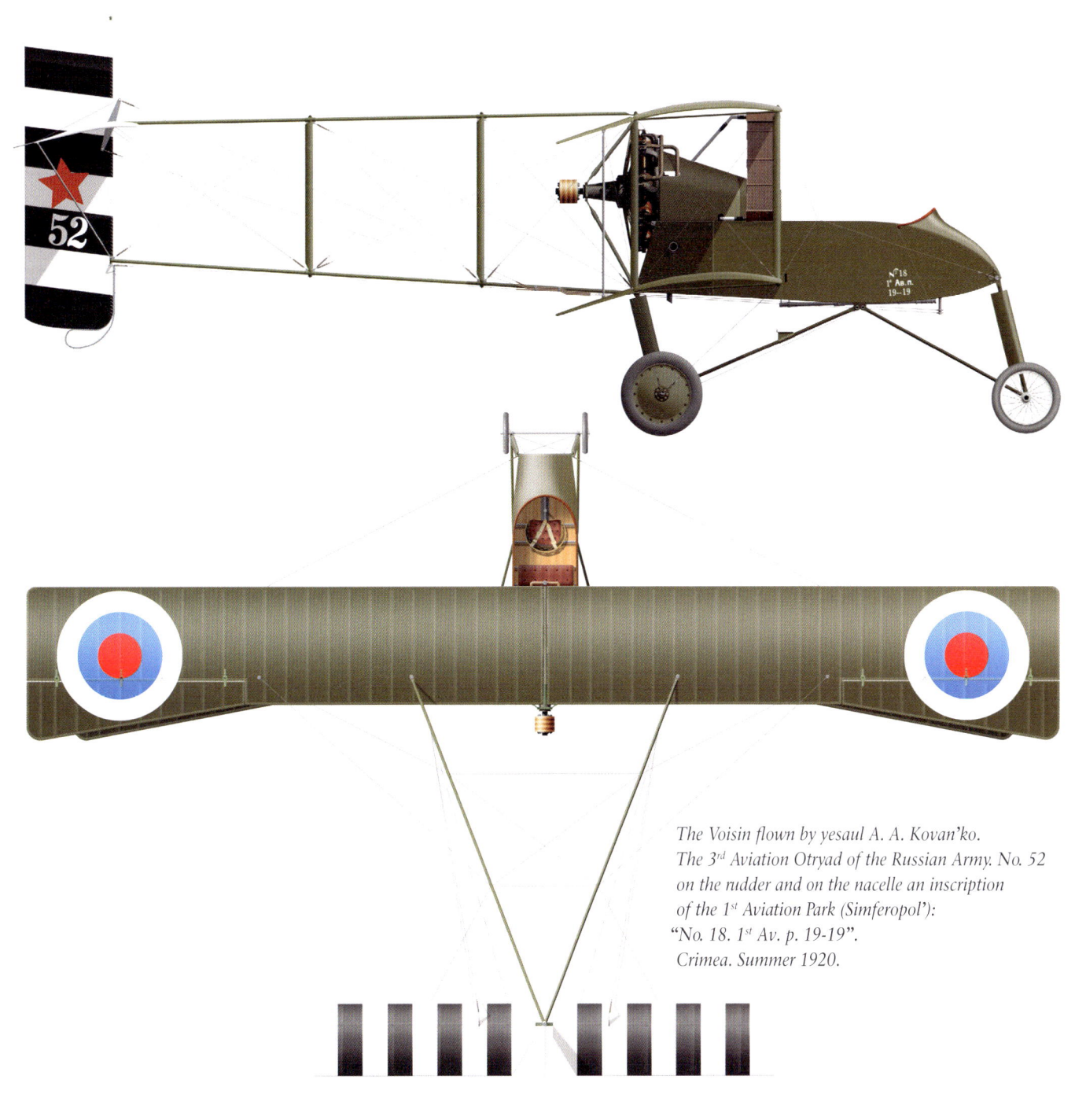

In early June one Voisin arrived at the front, to the 3rd Aviation Otryad. The reason why the entire tail surfaces of the machine were painted in white and black stripes (unlike the Nieuports with three-colour rudders) was probably simple: to make it immediately different from the Voisins of the Reds, which tended to appear in the Kerch' area. And friendly fighters could spot it from far away, without mistaking it for an enemy.

Let us return to the photos of captured machines in the Simferopol' park. Thanks to these photos a discovery was made. We have already discussed the first two types of national markings: 'old' Russian three-colour roundels and British (or French) ones. A third type of Crimean period recognition markings was discovered. Despite the fact that the markings on the wings were disfigured by retouching on the glass originals of the pictures, you can see the sequence of the bands in the markings: the outer white, then the blue and the red. By the way, in the former photo, behind the de Havilland you can see a part of the wing with an external white band of the recognition marking.

It is interesting that the same markings featured on AFSR armoured vehicles in 1919. For example, in order to identify their tanks and armoured cars, on 21 May 1920 (before the offensive), the following orders no. 15 were issued for the Crimean Combat Aviation Group:

> *"In the proposed operation, from among the group's otryads, the 4th and 5th will participate having their airfield at Armyansk town, and the 8th Otryad at the Chongar station. The tasks of the 4th and 5th Otryads united with the 1st Aviation Otryad under the general command of General Tkachëv or mine, are: [...] our tanks and armoured vehicles will have on their upper surfaces a recognition marking: a white roundel (1 arshin[30] diameter) or a small red circle with a broad white border of the same diameter."*[31]

Captured de Havillands in the Simferopol' park. The machine in the foreground was formerly used by the 4th Aviation Otryad of the Russian Army, as shown by the white rudder. Autumn 1920. (TsMVS)

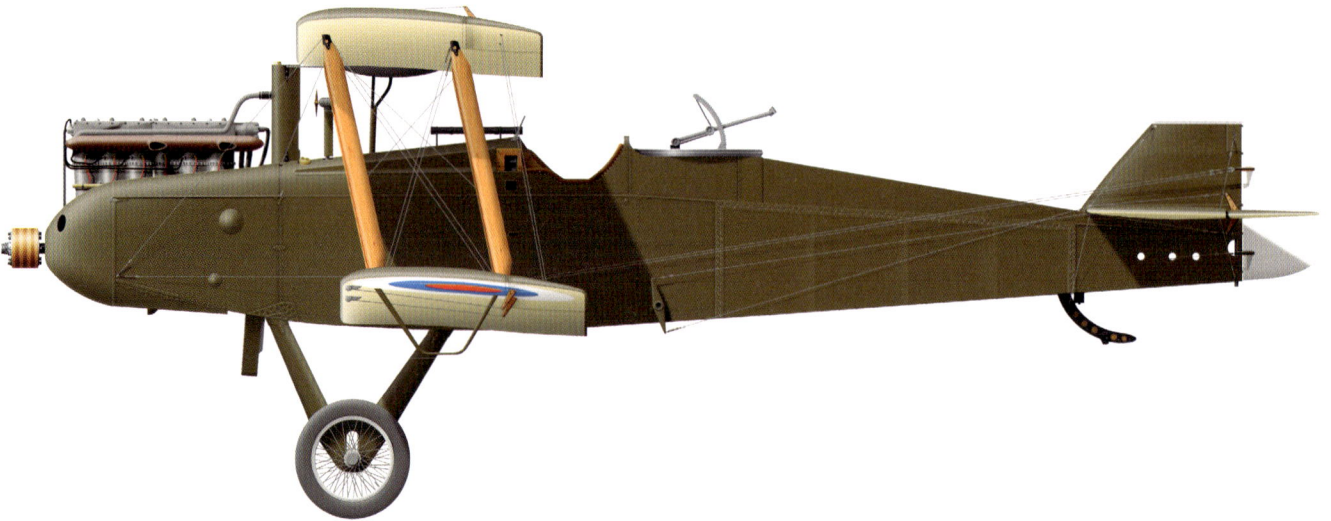

---

30   An old Russian unit of measurement. 1 arshin equals 0.711 metres.
31   RGVA. F. 40213. Op.1. D.1617. L. 9.

Austin armoured car of the 3rd series named "Ataman Bogayevskiy", photographed in Rostov in the summer of 1919. In addition to the Don marking (black triangle on a white disc) there is also a roundel in Russian colours (red-blue-white). (GA RF)

Bullock-Lombard armoured tractor manufactured in Novorossiysk. 1919. (GA RF)

As it is known, the aviaglav Tkachëv often flew on service trips to the front. Pokrovskiy also mentions this:

Both during periods of calm, and especially during the development of operations, general Tkachëv visited the front line otryads, usually by air, often personally leading combat group flights.[32]

He used various machines, a Nieuport, de Havilland or Sopwith.

One of his de Havillands is known, British serial no. D620. In the park, however, only the digits 620 were left. *General-mayor* Tkachëv fought in it as part of the 1st Aviation Otryad 'general Alekseyev' during the defeat of the Zhloba Corps in June 1920. Apparently, the aviaglav then continued to fly no. 620, since this machine was no longer listed as part of the 1st Otryad. It remains unknown what the colour scheme of the rudder on Tkachëv's aeroplane was.

---

32 Pokrovskiy S. "Rabota beloy aviatsii v Krymu i Severnoy Tavrii v 1920 godu", "Vestnik Vozdushnogo Flota", Moscow, No. 13/1922 p. 9.

> 11 September 1920
>
> Head of the Red Air Force of the South-Western Front.
> Secret, into their own hands.
>
> Announcing the received information about Vrangel' aviation: Aviadarm Tkachëv, now general-mayor, takes direct part in flights and has been awarded the Order of St Nicholas for these. Tkachëv is flying a Sopwith, **painted white with black stripes on the fuselage, wings and tail**. The Vrangel' army now has 4 otryads, made up of 8 otryads, and have up to 30 aeroplanes. There are R.E.8s, de Havillands, Voisins and Nieuports. [...].
>
> The younger Hartmann is listed as having been shot by the Bolsheviks. A mass of pilots serve in infantry for lack of vacancies in aviation. This information is credible, it is desirable to hunt for Tkachëv.
>
> *The Head of the Red Air Force, Red military pilot Sergeyev.**
>
> ** RGVA. F. 102. Op. 3. D. 743. L. 525.*

Captured de Havilland no. 620. It was flown in combat by general-mayor Tkachëv in June 1920. The machine was subsequently allocated to Kozlov, a pilot of the 24th Reconnaissance Aviation Otryad of the 1st Horse Army, who crashed it in January 1921. Simferopol', Autumn 1920. TsVMS

58

*The Sopwith 1½-Strutter
flown by general-mayor V. M. Tkachëv in 1920.
Reconstruction by A. V. Kazakov*

The origin of the image of the maple leaf with the inscription "Canada" can be explained by the fact that the aircraft had previously been earmarked for No. 2 (Canadian) Squadron, but instead was despatched to a British squadron in the Mediterranean. Perhaps the mechanic or pilot was Canadian.

According to information received from two sources, Tkachëv flew a Sopwith and a de Havilland. The above-described distinctive colour scheme of Aviaglav's aeroplanes may have the following explanation. In January 1917 Tkachëv's work "Material po taktike vozdushnogo boya" ("Material on Air Combat Tactics") was published, where in chapter 4 "Boy eskadril'yami" ("Combat by Flights") it was noted:

For easy identification of the commander's machine, it should be distinguished by recognition markings clearly visible from above, below and sides[33].

In conclusion of the story about the distinctive markings on aeroplanes of the Russian Army we provide some more photos.

The beautiful book by Vitaliy Zhumenko, "*Belaya armiya. Fotoportrety russkikh ofitserov 1917–1922*" ("The White Army. Photo-portraits of Russian officers 1917–1922") includes a photo of an aeroplane with a sharkmouth. The rudder colour is not visible, but there are British roundels on the wings. The rudder of the next machine is also finished in British colours. The same sharkmouth was also seen on the captured de Havillands of the 9th Kuban' Red Army, which was described in the Chapter 5.

There are a few pictures of captured Crimean de Havillands, which, rather than complement the general picture, simply add more questions.

For example, a photo from the archive of the former head of the *Pravoberezhnaya* (Right Bank) Aviation Group, Red military pilot I. K. Spatarel'. The date is difficult to establish, it can only be ascertained that the photo was not taken earlier than the autumn of 1920, when Arvatov became a pilot of the 13th Kazan' Aviation Otryad.

*De Havilland DH.9 flown by general-mayor V. M. Tkachëv in 1920.
Reconstruction by A. V. Kazakov*

---

33 Tkachëv V. M. "Material po taktike vozdushnogo boya" ("Material on Air Combat Tactics"), p. 49.

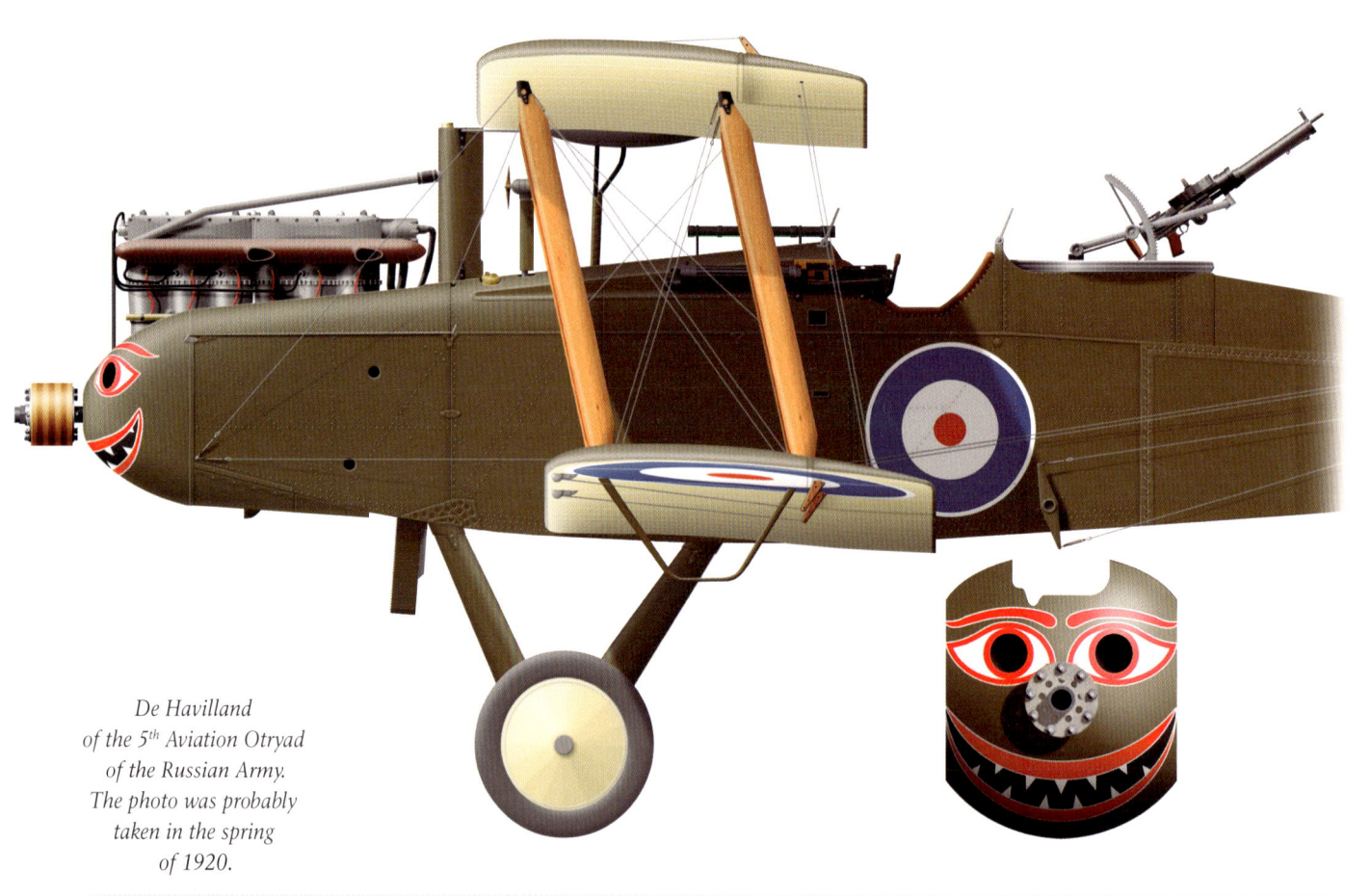

De Havilland of the 5th Aviation Otryad of the Russian Army. The photo was probably taken in the spring of 1920.

The date of the photo is important, since it could be assumed that this is the captured de Havilland of the 5th Aviation Otryad. In July 1920, when landing at one of the headquarters, military pilot shtabs-kapitan Kopanev broke the undercarriage of the machine, and during a sudden retreat the aeroplane was left to the Reds. Pokrovskiy writes about that case:

> *The reconnaissance sorties were usually accompanied by dropping a pennant with a notice to the corresponding corps or division headquarters. This method proved to be very reliable: up to 200 pennants were dropped throughout the work of the aviation group, all of which fell into the right hands. In the event of discovery of significant data at the front line of a formation, a landing was made at its headquarters, after which the aeroplane often took off for additional reconnaissance. This type of work drew aviation particularly close to the troops, while in technical terms, thanks to the flat nature of the terrain, it was not difficult to carry out and cases of damage in off-aerodrome landings were very rare. Only in one case, due to the extreme negligence*

60

of the division HQ, who demanded a landing on a square in a village and did not take the trouble to remove bystanders from it, the aeroplane suffered a serious accident and when the Whites left on the next night it was abandoned.[34]

A part of a drawing with a nude woman can be seen on the side of the captured aeroplane, behind the backs of the aviators. The photo may also have been taken in 1921, when the captured machine was received from the Simferopol' aviation park after the victory over Vrangel'. The 13th Otryad converted onto the de Havillands in January 1920. In general, it is not known who may have had the lady artwork applied on the fuselage.

Original caption: "With a captured DH.9 aeroplane with the Siddeley-Puma engine, captured from the Whites on the Vrangel' front in 1920. Left to right: head of the aviation of the 13th Army V. I. Korovin, air observer Dymze, commander of the 13th Kazan' Aviation Otryad P. Kh. Mezheraup, Red military pilot Yu. Arvatov, Red military pilot Yu. Krekis". (From the family archive of I. K. Spatarel')

A few more pictures of de Havillands with almost identically painted vertical tail were taken in 1921.
One of the machines, serial no. D2944, was in 1919 with the British No. 47 Squadron, and in 1920 fought in the aviation of the Russian Army (the otryad is unknown). In November the de Havilland was captured at the Simferopol' aviation park along with other Vrangel' aeroplanes. There it was overhauled and transferred in April 1921 to the 9th Reconnaissance Aviation Otryad. And in May the machine was handed over to the 13th Kazan' Otryad. The vertical tail of the machine was adorned with five black and four white diagonal stripes. Five-pointed red stars were applied on the wings.

Liberty-engined de Havilland (DH.9a) no. 185/13368. Aviation of the 1st Horse Army. 1921. (TsVMS)

---

34   Pokrovskiy S. "Rabota beloy aviatsii v Krymu i Severnoy Tavrii v 1920 godu", "Vestnik Vozdushnogo Flota", Moscow, No. 13/1922 p. 15.

De Havilland no. 2944 from the 13th Kazan' Aviation Otryad. Kharkiv, Summer 1921. (TsDAiK)

One more de Havilland is known, a DH.9a with a Liberty engine, the type being rare in the south of Russia. Its vertical tail was decorated with six black and six white diagonal stripes. It was overhauled at the GAZ No. 15 plant, this being the name of the former A. A. Anatra factory at Simferopol' during 1921–1922. It featured a factory mark (GAZ No. 15, 19–21, the rest illegible) close to the tail, and the number 185/13386 on the side. This was de Havilland DH.9 with the British serial no. H185. In June 1920 it was flown by the commander of the 1st Aviation Otryad of the Russian Army shtabs-kapitan A. A. Kovan'ko. And after the capture of Simferopol' and an overhaul at the factory, the machine went to the aviation of the 1st Horse Army.

Such diagonal stripes were similar to the 1920 version of the 12th Fighter Otryad markings familiar to us from Chapter 5. The difference was that the stripes were red, not black. In 1924, one of the otryads of the 3rd Fighter Aviation Escadrille also used red-and-white diagonal stripes.

Concluding the story about the insignia and markings of the Russian Army aviation, let us present one more photo of a captured de Havilland with a striped tail, apparently taken at the Duks plant. There are five dark and five light horizontal stripes on the vertical tail. It cannot be stated definitely that these striped tails were otryad markings of the Whites in their aviation in the Crimea and Northern Tavriya.

A captured de Havilland photographed in 1920 or 1921 at the Duks factory. (TsVMS)

Aviation of the North-Western Army

On 1 July 1919[35] the Northern Corps and other scattered Russian anti-Bolshevik formations stationed in the territory of the Pskov province and the Baltics were amalgamated to form the North-Western Army (NWA) under *general-leytenant* A. P. Rodzyanko.

From 8 July the Aviation Department of the NWA began forming, headed by *leytenant* V. A. fon Shtral'born (von Strahlborn). Two aviation otryads were formed on paper.

Through Lieutenant-General H. Gough, the head of all the Allied military missions in Finland and the Baltics, the army received six British R.E.8 aeroplanes, which had arrived in Revel by 5 August 1919.

In early August the 'Most Luminous Duke Liven' Aviation Otryad, under the command of *rotmistr* V. Andrzhevskiy, arrived in Narva with two Nieuport 24*bis* machines.

Thus, the three aviation otryads of the NWA were armed with six British R.E.8s (two of them lay, unserviceable, in storage in Tallinn) and two French Nieuport 24*bis*.

On 16 October 1919 units of the NWA occupied Krasnoye Selo, close to where the Naval School of Advanced Flying was located. Rich trophies were captured: two Nieuport 10 training biplanes, one Lebedev Al'batros and two or three Nieuport 17 fighters.

At the end of October, 14 officer pilots arrived in Narva, the so-called aviation group commanded by military pilot *gvardii kapitan* G. Sakhnovskiy. The 18 aeroplanes promised by the British failed to arrive.

One of the new arrivals, military pilot *shtabs-kapitan* B. V. Sergiyevskiy, recalled:

> … England sent some of its most obsolete aeroplanes, with which we had to organise the air forces of a new army. I got an R.E.8 aeroplane, which I had seen in England in museums only, since this type was considered obsolete already at the beginning of 1916. It had an air-cooled engine with in-line cylinders. The front cylinders were always too cold, and the rear ones always too hot.
>
> […]
>
> Our aviation equipment of the North-Western Army was so poor that we could not actually do any useful work and from time to time we volunteered for the infantry, fighting as ordinary soldiers, because against each man in the White Army there were at least 25 or 30 in the Red. But, in spite of all this, the North-Western Army won victories in every battle. We advanced quickly, and soon were at the very gates of Petersburg. The domes of the churches and Saint Isaac's Cathedral glittering in the rays of the sun could already be seen.
>
> […]
>
> The air forces of the North-Western Army were not placed in the Estonian concentration camp. We could walk freely wherever we wanted and do anything as we pleased, and only our aeroplanes were confiscated… in Reval [Tallinn]…"[36]

The seal of the NWA Aviation Group, used until February 1920.

---

35 Dates are quoted according to the new style (Gregorian calendar).
36 B. V. Sergiyevskiy. "Vospominaniya" ("Memoirs"). New York, 1975 p. 88–90.

On 3 November the army left Gatchina, retreating to Yamburg and Gdov, and the aviation was concentrated in Narva again. General-leytenant Glazenap ordered on 1 December 1919 to "*concentrate unnecessary automobile and aviation assets in the depot-base in Reval*", and on 9 December the aeroplanes remaining in Narva were combined into a divizion. The three otryads were merged to form two, a fighter and a reconnaissance one. On 22 January 1920 orders were signed to liquidate the NWA. Its fate was shared by its small aviation component. All aeroplanes of the NWA were acquired by Estonia.[37]

A hangar in Tallinn. Left to right: in the corner there are remnants of a fuselage with the Estonian recognition marking (blue-black-white triangle), then the right lower wing of an M-9 hydroplane with a red star inscribed in the inner of two red rings, then the wings of a Lebed' 12, behind it a wing of an R.E.8 with a British roundel. On the right a German Friedrichshafen floatplane. Estonia, Winter 1919/1920. (ERA)

Former aeroplanes of the North-Western Army (except for the Friedrichshafen floatplane on the right in the photo). Left to right: Nieuport 10 captured in the Naval School of Air Combat at Krasnoye Selo, with the Duks roundel and the flag of St Andrew, a Nieuport 10, a fuselage of an R.E.8 with a white cross of St George (the marking of the North-Western Army Aviation), a Nieuport 17 or 24bis and an Albatros. Tallinn, Estonia, Winter 1919/1920. (ERA)

37　Khairulin M. A "Aviatsiya Severo-Zapadnoy armii (oktyabr' 1918 – yanvar' 1920 g.)" ("Aviation of the North-Western Army (October 1918 – January 1920)") // "Belaya Gvardiya" almanac No. 7/2003 p. 213–220.

R.E.8 serial no. E203 of the 2nd Aviation Otryad of the North-Western Army. The white cross of St George on the side was the recognition marking of the North-Western Army Aviation. Autumn 1919.

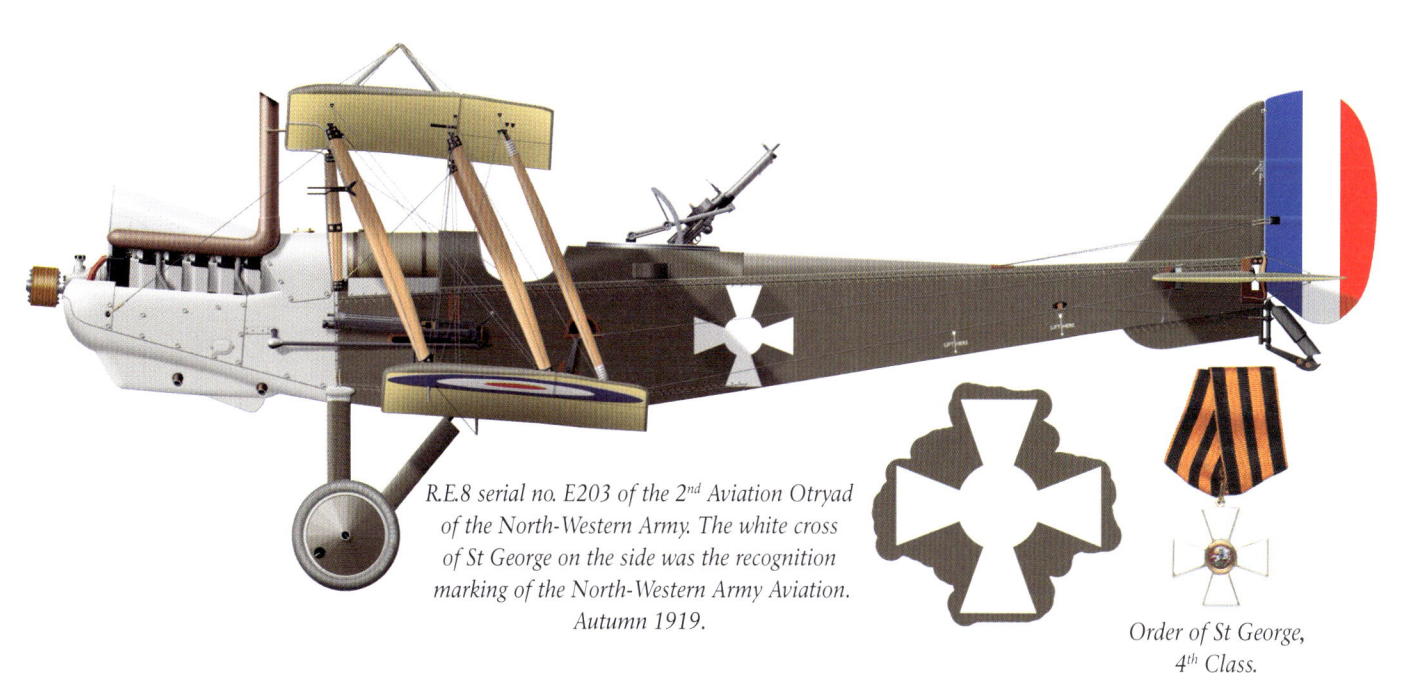

Order of St George, 4th Class.

The fuselage of a Nieuport 24bis used as a hearse. Rings of the old recognition marking can be seen showing through the colours of the Estonian flag (blue-black-white) on the rudder. Notably, unlike the traditional Russian aviation marking (a red-blue-white roundel), the order of colours is as follows: outer white, then blue and central red, as used in the aviation of the Russian Army. Tallinn, Early 1920s. (From the collection of T. Kitvel')

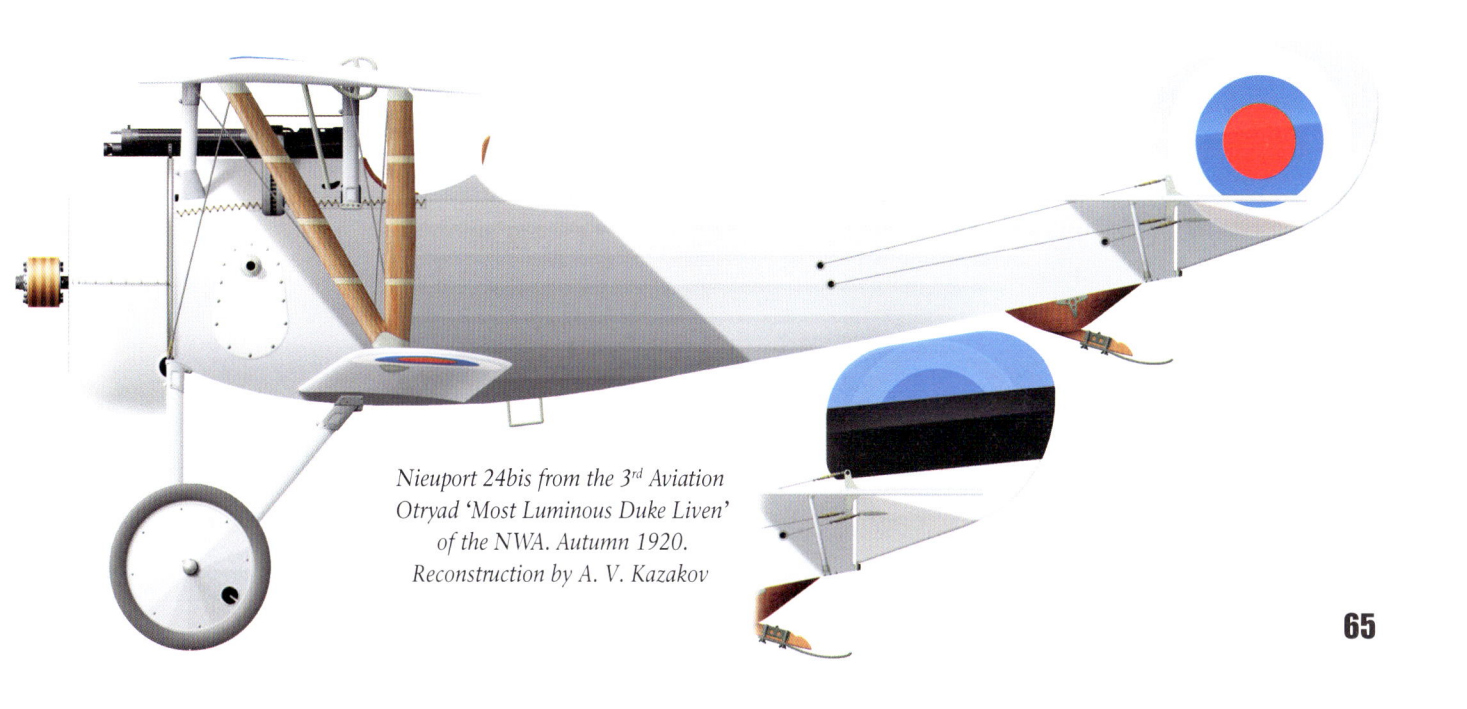

Nieuport 24bis from the 3rd Aviation Otryad 'Most Luminous Duke Liven' of the NWA. Autumn 1920. Reconstruction by A. V. Kazakov

A line-up of Estonian Air Force aeroplanes. On the left are Nieuports of the former NWA aviation with rudders and elevators painted in their national colours. The 'ten' with the Estonian number 51 shows a rectangular spot near the cockpit in place of the flag of St Andrew and an Estonian marking on top of the old roundel. Tallinn, 1923. (From the collection of T. Kitvel')

On the left are two Duks-built Nieuport 17s with the blue-black-white triangles on the side. These machines were earlier used by the NWA aviation. Tartu, 1923. (From the collection of T. Kitvel')

The accident of Nieuport 24bis no. 4306, Estonian no. 43, of pilot Arro. A roundel, an obliterated old recognition marking, can be seen on the upper wing. This machine was previously assigned to N. P. Pushkel', a pilot of the 1st Latvian Aviation Otryad who had defected on 9 May 1919. The pilot flew it with the Aviation Otryad 'Most Luminous Duke Liven', then the machine was used by the Estonians. Tartu, 21 August 1922. (From the collection of T. Kitvel')

What kind of recognition markings were applied on the NWA aeroplanes? No photos of the captured Nieuport 24*bis* of the 'Most Luminous Duke Liven' Otryad survive. It must be added that these machines had previously displayed red stars, since on 9 May 1919 pilots of the 1st Latvian Aviation Otryad had flown them from Riga to the enemy side.[38]

The North-Western R.E.8s had British markings, which can be seen in photographs related to the Estonian period.

In the photographs taken during the winter of 1919–1920 in the hangar of the naval fortress of the Tsar Peter the Great in Tallinn, the former machines of the NWA aviation can be seen. For example, Nieuport 10 retained the factory-applied markings (Duks roundels).

Light signs of the motif of the Order of Saint George the Great Martyr and Victor are clearly distinguishable on the fuselage of the R.E.8! It is not impossible that his motif served as the recognition marking for the North-Western Army aviation. Due to absence of orders for the NWA aviation, all the orders for the Army for the entire period of its short existence were inspected, and no mention of markings of the aviation was found.

It can also be assumed that the aeroplane was flown from November 1919 by the commander of the 2nd Aviation Otryad of the NWA, *shtabs-kapitan* B. V. Sergiyevskiy, a holder of the Order of Saint George. However, the method of applying the white cross of St George on the fuselage instead of the British roundel means it is possible that this was the recognition marking of the NWA aviation.

Photographs of the Estonian period were inspected in search of previous markings of NWA aeroplanes. One of these was unexpectedly discovered to show the former NWA aviation marking! The roundel consisted of a white outer ring, then the same width of blue, and a red centre.

Aviation of the Western Volunteer Army

In January 1919 the Libava Volunteer Otryad was formed in Liepaja (Libava), under the command of *rotmistr* Duke Liven, which reported to the Supreme Headquarters of the Baltic *Landswehr*. Another Russian volunteer unit was formed at the Salzwedel camp in Germany: "Independent partisan otryad 'general-ot-kavalerii graf Keller'" under *polkovnik* P. R. Bermondt, who arrived at Jelgava (Mitava) in Courland in June.

Along with Bermont's unit, the otryad of the former *polkovnik* of the Tsar's *Gendarmerie Vyrgolich* was also organised at the same time in Salzwedel, with the active participation of Senator A. Bel'gard. Initially it numbered 400 men, but a significant influx of prisoners of war quickly increased it to 1,050 troops in February, and in May it numbered about 1,200. On 6 June, in Jelgava, this unit, together with that of Bermont, was included in the Western Corps of the North-Western Army of gen. Yudenich, who was nominally represented there by *polkovnik* Liven in his capacity of Commander of all Russian units on the Courland Front. In view of this, Bermondt's otryad acquired the new name of "Partisan otryad 'general-ot-kavalerii graf Keller'". When, on 9 July, orders were received from general Yudenich to advance to meet the North-Western Army on the Narva Front, *polkovniks* Bermondt and Vyrgolich refused to carry out the orders, arguing that the forming of their otryads had not been completed yet. Moreover, the departure of Liven's otryad to Yudenich (between 18 and 26 July) gave Bermondt and Vyrgolich the opportunity to withdraw their units from the Western Corps on 18 July and to reorganise the "Partisan otryad" into the "Western Volunteer Corps 'general-ot-kavalerii graf Keller'", and a week later, into the "1st Western Volunteer Corps 'general graf Keller'". Vyrgolich's otryad, in turn, acquired the new name of the "2nd Western Volunteer Corps" (*II. Freiwilliger Westkorps Oberst Wirgolitsch*) and on 26 July the Plastun Brigade was expanded into the 1st Plastun Division with a two-regiment establishment, although by 12 August only the 1st Plastun Regiment had attained full combat readiness. Russian soldiers were dressed in German uniforms with Tsarist army cockades. 3,095 German soldiers had already joined both Russian corps' by the end of July and the number continued to grow daily, which in turn allowed them to be merged to form the Western Volunteer Army (WVA) under P. R. Bermondt, who now called himself Duke Avalov.

In early October, German units joined the Army: the Iron Division, the German Legion, the Plehwe *Freikorps*, the Diebitsch Corps.

Avalov demanded that the Latvian government let his army through the territory of Latvia to the 'Bolshevik Front' and began moving from Jelgava towards Daugavpils. The Government of Latvia replied with a refusal. On 8 October forward units of the Bermondt-Avalov's Western Volunteer Army moved towards Riga. In mid-November, Latvian units went on the offensive and Bermondt's army began to retreat towards the borders of Prussia. In early December the army was allowed to enter the territory of Germany.

---

38   For more details of this episode see M. Khairulin's article "Iz istorii aviatsii nezavisimoy Latvii. 1918–1940" ("From the history of aviation of independent Latvia. 1918–1940"), published in "Mir Aviatsii" magazine No. 2/1996. Pp. 2–7.

Halberstadt C.L.IV no. C.9432/18 (Rol.)
from the German FFA 425.
Lithuania, Šiauliai, August 1919.

Orders to the 'graf Keller' Western Volunteer Corps No. 17.

23 August 1919
town of Mitava [Jelgava]

I have approved the following recognition markings on aeroplanes in the Aviation Otryad of the Corps entrusted to me.

On the port lifting plane: an eight-pointed cross underneath and on top.
On the starboard lifting plane: a roundel of national colours underneath and on top.
On the tail: roundels of national colours on both sides, and an eight-pointed cross on the right and the left side of the aeroplane fuselage.

Corps Commander Polkovnik Bermondt*

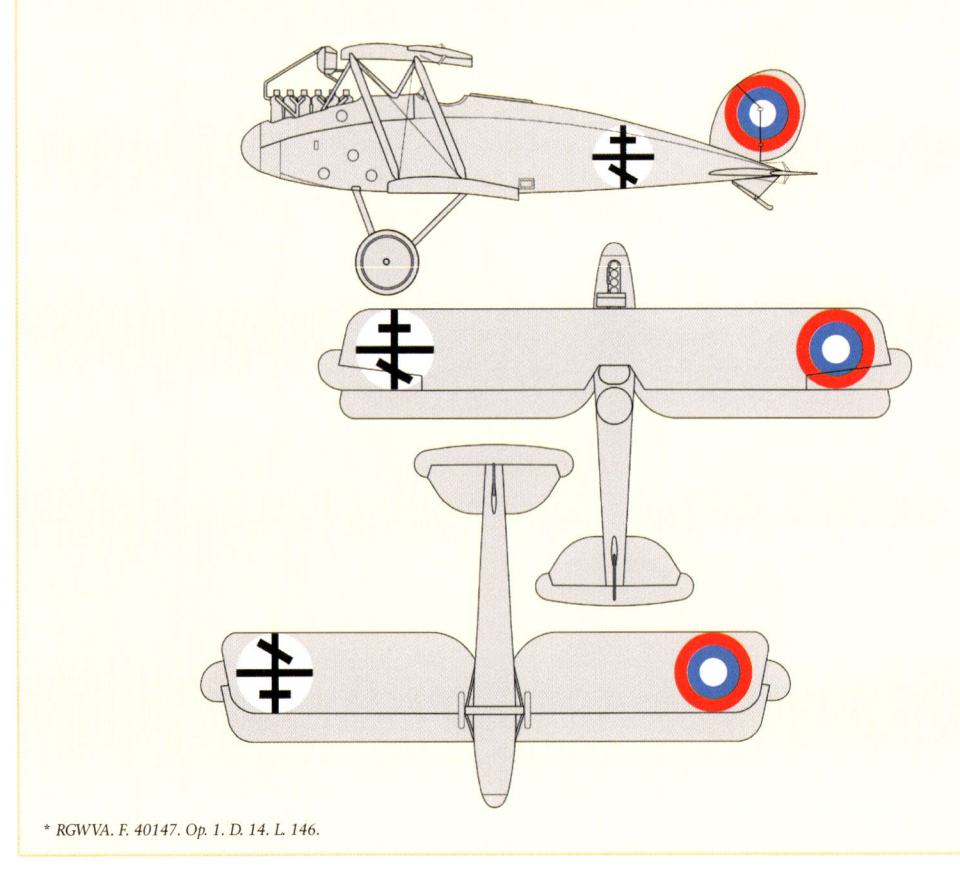

* *RGWVA. F. 40147. Op. 1. D. 14. L. 146.*

68

*Albatros C.XV no. C.7818/18
from the Plastun Aviation Otryad (no. unknown)
of the Western Volunteer Corps 'graf Keller' of the WVA,
which took an active part in the battles for Riga.
Jelgava, Latvia Autumn 1919.
Reconstruction by A. V. Kazakov*

*A photograph of an abandoned and broken fuselage, which clearly shows the Bermondt markings, taken in Riga in 1920. Albatros C.XV no. C.7818/18, which had belonged to the aviation of the Western Volunteer Corps 'graf Keller', was probably damaged during combat. The machine, which was delivered to the Latvian aviation, was decommissioned in December 1919 as "not repairable". Two aeroplanes of this type also served in the Lithuanian aviation.
(Kara muzejs)*

German aviation units were also present in the Baltics after the end of the war with Russia. Several of Bermondt's aviation units were formed on their basis.[39] Naturally, all the aeroplanes were of German manufacture and displayed their 'native' recognition markings, and only a few 'Russian' units had their own emblems, as will be discussed below.

The 1st (Corps) Aviation Otryad of the Western Volunteer Corps 'general-ot-kavalerii graf Keller' became the first of Bermondt's aviation unit, which started forming in June 1919 with the FFA 424[40] at Auce (Alt Autz) in Courland. It was commanded by *podpolkovnik* B. N. Firsov, who in late July became the head of the aviation HQ of the corps, and later of the Western Volunteer Army. Firsov was replaced in command of the 1st Otryad by military pilot *podpolkovnik* A. N. Livotov. The 12-aeroplane (according to the establishment) otryad had mixed staff: the majority were Germans and only a small part were Russians. This unit was called *Russische Detachement Graf Keller* in German documents.

Based on the FFA 424, the 2nd Plastun Aviation Otryad was also formed. It was commanded by *Leutnant* von Boddin, an FFA 424 pilot. The 2nd Plastun Otryad was based in Mitau and took an active part in combats in the autumn of 1919. This detachment was initially not part of the Plastun aviation divizions (which will be discussed below), and from 18 September it reported directly to the WVA aviation HQ. Both detachments formed the Aviation Park of the 'graf Keller' Corps. On 31 August the Park with the 1st Otryad was transferred to Šiauliai in Lithuania.

39 This section uses information from the manuscript of M. Bukhman, "Wings in the Baltic Skies in 1919" and RGVA, f. 40147 "Zapadnaya Dobrovol'cheskaya armiya" ("Western Volunteer Army").
40 Freiwilligen Flieger Abteilung – Volunteer Aviation Detachment.

German aeroplanes captured by the Lithuanians on the slipway at Kaunas. 1920. (Plieno Sparnai)

Captured Bermondt's Albatroses (types, right to left: B.II, C.XV, C.XV, D.III and C.I), photographed on the slipway at Kaunas in 1920. A part of the Bermondt marking, an eight-pointed cross in a white disc, can be seen on one of the C.XVs. (Plieno Sparnai)

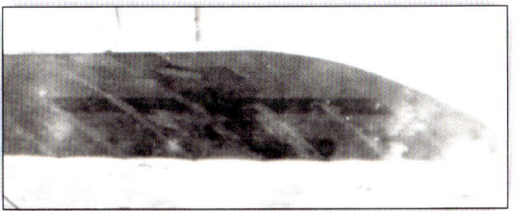

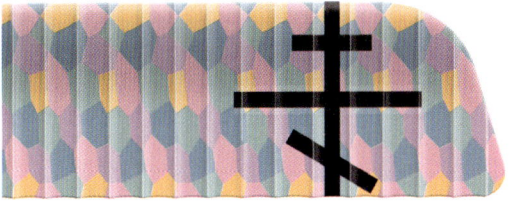

One of two machines (no. C.7817/18), restored in a Lithuanian aviation park. It was first flown following the repairs in the spring of 1921. Without a doubt, both machines had belonged, like the 'Latvian' no. C.7818/18, to one of the aviation otryads of the Western Volunteer Corps 'graf Keller' of the WVA. On the port wing it displays the marking announced in the Corps' orders no. 17: "on the port lifting plane: an eight-pointed cross on the bottom and top".

On 28 July 1919 the other German detachments (FFA 425 and FFA 433) that were at Auce at that time were combined to form the Courland Aviation Park (*Flugpark Kurland*), which was relocated to the Ginkūnai estate north of Šiauliai on 8 August. From about September the Park became known as the 2nd Plastun. The Aviation Park of the 'graf Keller' Corps received the number 1 (the Germans called it in their documents the *Flugpark des russischen Freiwilligen-Westkorps "Graf Keller"* or the *I Plastuner Flugpark*). *Podpolkovnik* Vil'kovuyskiy was the head of the Russian park.

There are surviving orders for recognition markings, which, however, only applied to the otryads of the 1st Aviation Divizion, and also, possibly, to Vyrgolich's otryad. In the remaining divizions, the existing German markings were preserved, as evidenced by all surviving photographic material.

The pedantic Germans repeated the corps orders, specifying the description of the markings: Russian Baltic cross on a white field (*russische Baltenkreuz im weissem Felde*) and national colour roundels (Kokarden in den russischen Nationalfarben (weiss-blau-rot))[41]

So, the aeroplanes of the 1st and 2nd Plastun Aviation Otryads, and possibly of the 1st and 2nd Aviation Divizions, which were part of the 'graf Keller' Western Volunteer Corps, which subsequently joined the WVA, displayed the Russian recognition markings mentioned in the order no. 17 above.

Only one photographic confirmation of the published order has survived to this day.

However, a series of photographs taken in Kaunas in 1920 survives in Lithuania. On some captured Bermondt aeroplanes an eight-pointed cross in a white circle can be seen. Another Bermondt cross was found on the lower wing of an Albatross in one of the images.

In September 1919, all the German aviation units left in the Baltics were reformed into four Plastun aviation divizions, consisting initially of nine Plastun aviation otryads and two Plastun aviation parks. In October, the total number of aviation otryads was increased to eleven. According to Bermondt, his aviation numbered 120 aeroplanes in October 1919.

For example, on 5 September 1919, the OdB of the 'graf Keller' Western Volunteer Corps aviation was as follows:

Unit name	Number of aeroplanes	Notes
Corps aviation HQ	1	Commander – podpolkovnik Firsov
I Plastun Aviation Otryad	6	
II Plastun Aviation Otryad	32	
III Plastun Aviation Otryad	–	During formation at the Aviation Park
IV Plastun Aviation Otryad	–	During formation at the Aviation Park
1st Aviation Divizion HQ	–	During formation at the Aviation Park
2nd Aviation Divizion composed of V, VI, VII and VIII Plastun Aviation Otryads	46	
Total	**85**	**With 48 pilots and 21 observers**

41   LVVA. 6033/1/180/61.

> **Orders of the Western Volunteer Army No. 1**
>
> **"12" September 1919**
>
> **town of Mitava [Jelgava]**
>
> The Army Commander has ordered:
>
> § 2.
>
> I announce for the attention the features of aeroplanes of the 2nd Western Volunteer Corps:
>
> On the left side (in the direction of flight) of the upper and lower wing, and also on the right and left sides of the fuselage, the marking of the 2nd Western Volunteer Corps, i.e. a white cross in a blue field. On the right side of the upper and lower wing, as well as on both sides of the lateral control, the Russian national roundels (white-blue-red).
>
> *For the Chief of Staff,*
> *Polkovnik Chaykovskiy**
>
> RGVA. F. 40147. Op. 1. D. 19. L. 154.

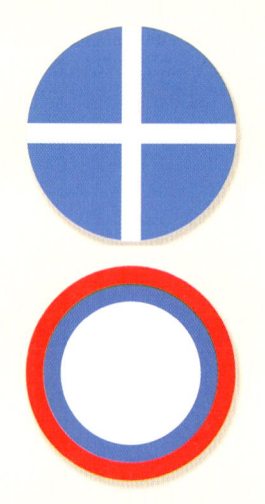

Halberstadt from the German FFA 426. Lithuania, Šiauliai Summer 1919.

Aeroplanes of the 2nd Plastun Aviation Divizion (Fliegergeschwader Weinschenk, FFA 426), captured by the Lithuanians on 22 November 1919. In the photographs of the fuselages not yet covered with tarpaulin, one can recognise Fokker D.VII and Halberstadt CL.II. Lithuania, Radviliškis. (From the collection of M. Bukhman)

Albatros D.III no. D.5160/17 (OAW) of the Western Volunteer Army aviation. The aeroplane was rebuilt and used by the Lithuanian aviation with code no. 1. Reconstruction by A. V. Kazakov

A train with captured Bermondt's aeroplanes. An Albatros D.III is on the first car, an LVG C.V on the next one. All machines display German crosses. Lithuania, Kaunas, 13 December 1919. (From the collection of M. Bukhman)

On 18 September Vyrgolich's Aviation Otryad (without aeroplanes), also known as the "1st Kolchak Aviation Otryad", and the 5th Plastun Aviation Otryad of the 2nd Division, all became part of the newly formed 1st Plastun Aviation Divizion. The unit was deployed in the area of Šiauliai, and it was led by an observer pilot from FFA 426, *Leutnant* Arimand.

It is known that Vyrgolich's corps 'sat' in the area of Šiauliai and the otryad mentioned above was formed for it, as well as for the 'graf Keller' Western Corps. The Plastun number of the otryad is unknown, perhaps there never was one, since it was simply referred to in documents as "Vyrgolich's aviation otryad" or "1st Kolchak Aviation Otryad". The orders about recognition markings have survived. It is impossible to say for sure whether the orders applied to all aviation otryads of the 1st Aviation Divizion, as the 5th Plastun Otryad transferred from the 2nd Aviation Divizion.

The 2nd Plastun Aviation Divizion, also known as the Weinschenk Aviation Regiment (*Fliegergeschwader Weinschenk*), was established on the basis of the FFA 426. The divizion consisted of two active aviation otryads (6th and 8th) and two at the stage of forming (the 5th, transferred to the 1st Aviation Divizion, and the 7th). The divizion was based in the Lithuanian territory at Radviliškis and served the German Legion, although it had earlier belonged to the 'graf Keller' Western Corps.

The German FFA 424 was expanded in October into the 3rd Plastun Aviation Divizion composed of the 1st and 2nd Plastun Aviation Otryads (commanders *Hauptmann* Erdenberger and *Leutnant* von Boddin), tactically subordinated to the 1st and 2nd Plastun Regiments respectively. The command of the 3rd Aviation Divizion, like the former FF 424, was retained by *Oberleutnant* Martin. The flying staff remained German and transferred to the Western Volunteer Army on the basis of a collective agreement between Martin and Bermondt in August.

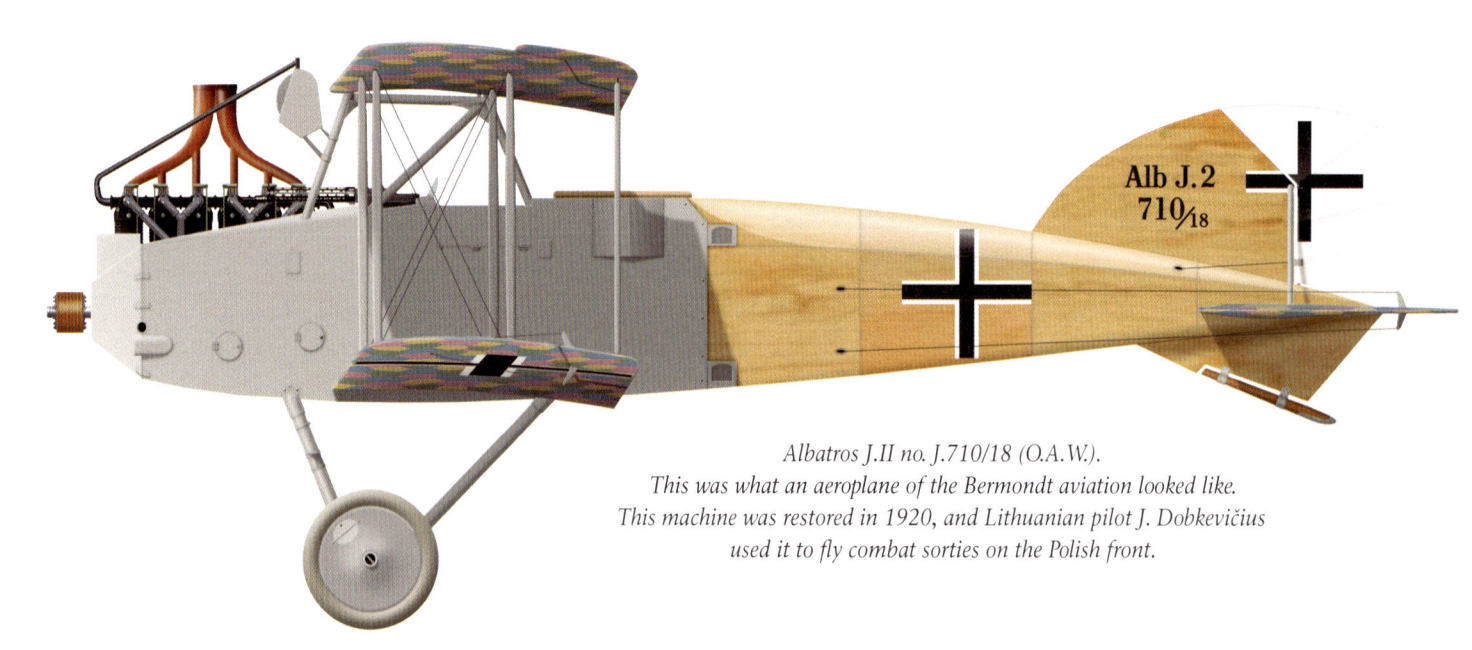

Albatros J.II no. J.710/18 (O.A.W.).
This was what an aeroplane of the Bermondt aviation looked like.
This machine was restored in 1920, and Lithuanian pilot J. Dobkevičius
used it to fly combat sorties on the Polish front.

Captured Bermondt's Albatroses (J.II and B.II no. B.1751/17) with German crosses. Lithuania, Kaunas, December 1919. (From the collection of M. Bukhman)

Captured aeroplanes of the Bermondt aviation. Fokker D.VII fuselages with German crosses can be seen. Lithuania, Radviliškis, November 1919. (From the collection of M. Bukhman)

Albatros B.II no. B.616/17 (Mer), which had belonged to the aviation of the Western Volunteer Army. The aeroplane was inspected in Riga in December 1919 and declared airworthy following an overhaul. The machine served in a Latvian aviation school with the code no. 5. (Kara muzejs)

After two aviation detachments of the Sachsenberg Regiment (*Kampfgeschwader Sachsenberg*) were recalled into East Prussia, only the reconnaissance detachment (FFA 413) remained at the Petersfeld airfield in the area of the Courland town of Dobele. This was expanded into the 4th Plastun Aviation Divizion (*4 Fliegerdivision*) under the unchanged command of *Leutnant* Sachsenberg. In October the 4th Divizion was part of the German Legion.

The divizion allocation of the 3rd, 4th, 9th, 10th and 11th Plastun Aviation Otryads has not been established, but they were distributed between the 4th Aviation Divizion and the units of the Iron Division. In August the Iron Division had 16 aeroplanes (FFA 427 and the 101st Artillery Aviation Unit), which were stationed at Jelgava.

After the defeat of Bermondt, Lithuania and Latvia received a total of about 100 German aeroplanes, mostly in a deplorable condition. The Lithuanians managed to capture almost complete aeroplanes from the FFA 426 (30 machines) at Radviliškis. But the machines of both Plastun aviation parks from the Ginkūnai estate near Šiauliai were shipped to Prussia in early November, although thanks to the intervention of General Niessel, and then under pressure from the British, they were returned to the Lithuanians. The Germans returned the aeroplanes, but in Königsberg they placed hand grenades in these, damaging the old machines, already broken in accidents, even more. Nevertheless, the Lithuanians managed to restore several machines from this batch, which then took part in the Lithuanian-Polish war in 1920.

More than twenty of Bermondt's aeroplanes were acquired by Latvia. Most of the machines were restored, and they successfully served in Latvian aviation.

Aviation of the White forces in the North of Russia

In March 1918 the British landed in Murmansk, initiating a long-term intervention by Allied forces in the north of Russia. The former allies seized the most important ports, Murmansk and Arkhangel'sk, and fought against the Bolsheviks until October 1919. Without mentioning the aviation of the British expeditionary force, the story of the White air formations in the north of Russia would be incomplete. It was only after the withdrawal of the allies that the 1st Aviation Otryad of the Northern Front and the Murmansk Aviation Divizion were formed, which were part of the Russian forces of the Northern Front.

Slavo-British Aviation Corps

In the first half of 1918 Russian officers, including pilots who did not recognise the peace with Germany and did not want to fight on the side of the Red Army, made their way north to Murmansk and Arkhangel'sk, where allied troops were already stationed. The Slavo-British Legion was formed, and at the end of June the formation of the Slavo-British Aviation Corps within its structure commenced. The corps (SBAC) had both British and Russian pilots.

In June 1918 *polkovnik* A. A. Kozakov and his colleagues managed to get all the way from Moscow to Murmansk. He was given the task of forming the 1st Otryad (No. 1 Squadron SBAC), which consisted of a pair of Nieuports and several Sopwiths.

The magazine "Nasha Stikhiya" wrote about the formation of the otryad:

> *Colonel Mound suggested that our pilots form a "Slavo-British Aviation Corps", because at the time the English have formed in our North something like their colonial troops: they rebuilt Russian military forces in their own way, introduced their posts, appointed Englishmen to senior command posts, etc. The units thus formed existed on English account and used English allowances. The proposal of Col. Mound was accepted.*

Two Nieuport 17s and a Sopwith collected for the 1st Otryad of the Slavo-British Aviation Corps. Arkhangel'sk, Summer 1918. (From the collection of V. P. Kulikov)

*French Sopwith 1½-Strutter.
No. 1 Squadron of the Slavo-British Aviation Corps.
'Railway' front, September 1918.*

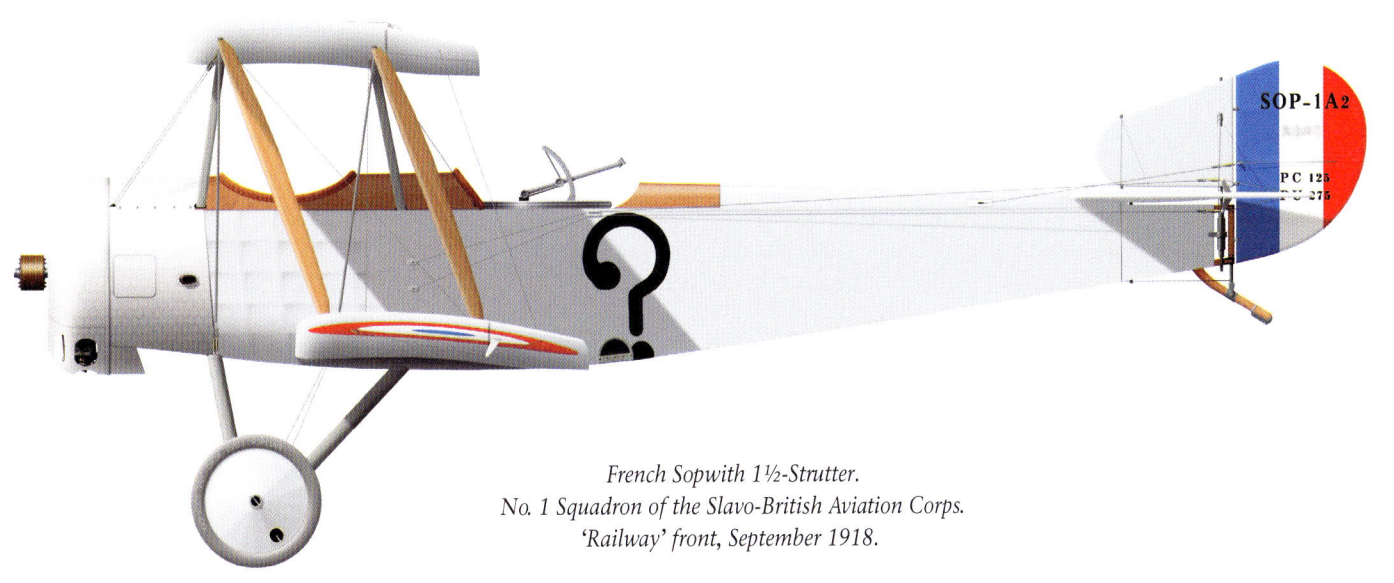

A French Sopwith 1½-Strutter. Such silver machines with Russian three-colour roundels applied were supplied by France to Russia. Arkhangel'sk, Summer 1918. (TsDAiK)

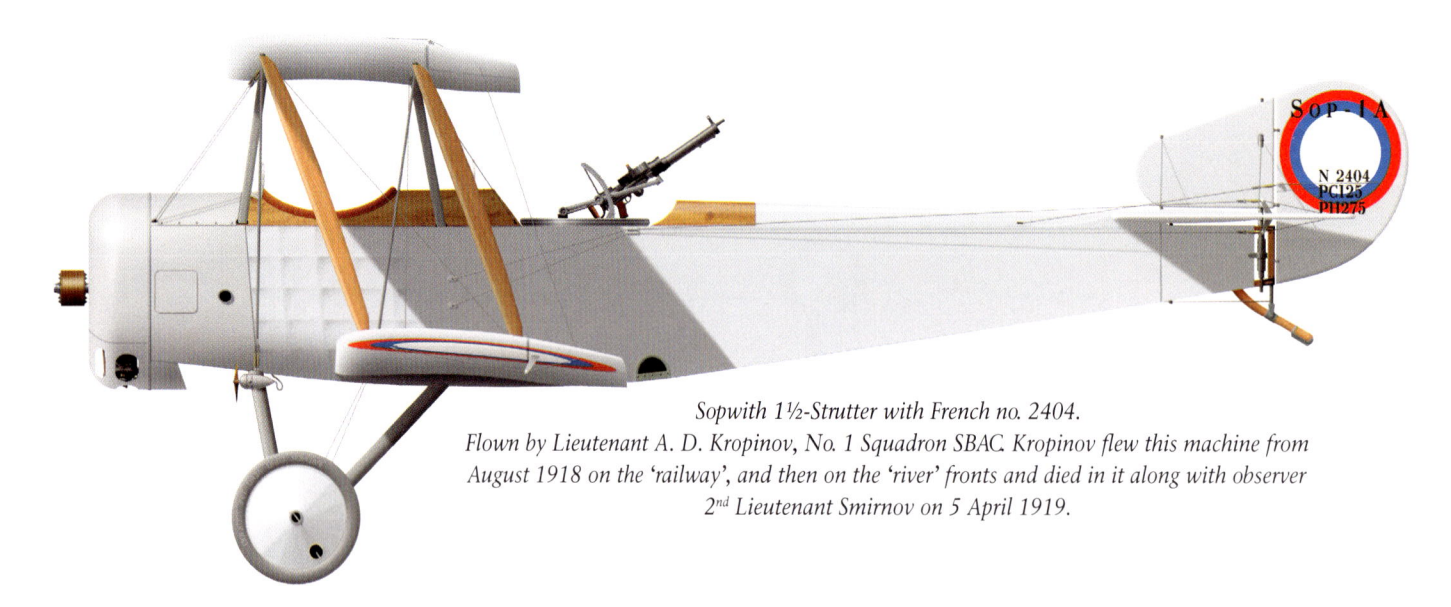

*Sopwith 1½-Strutter with French no. 2404.
Flown by Lieutenant A. D. Kropinov, No. 1 Squadron SBAC. Kropinov flew this machine from
August 1918 on the 'railway', and then on the 'river' fronts and died in it along with observer
2nd Lieutenant Smirnov on 5 April 1919.*

*Departure of Captain Kozakov, the Commander of No. 1 Squadron SBAC. The Sopwith retained Russian recognition markings.
'River' front, Bereznik December 1918.
(From the collection of V. P. Kulikov)*

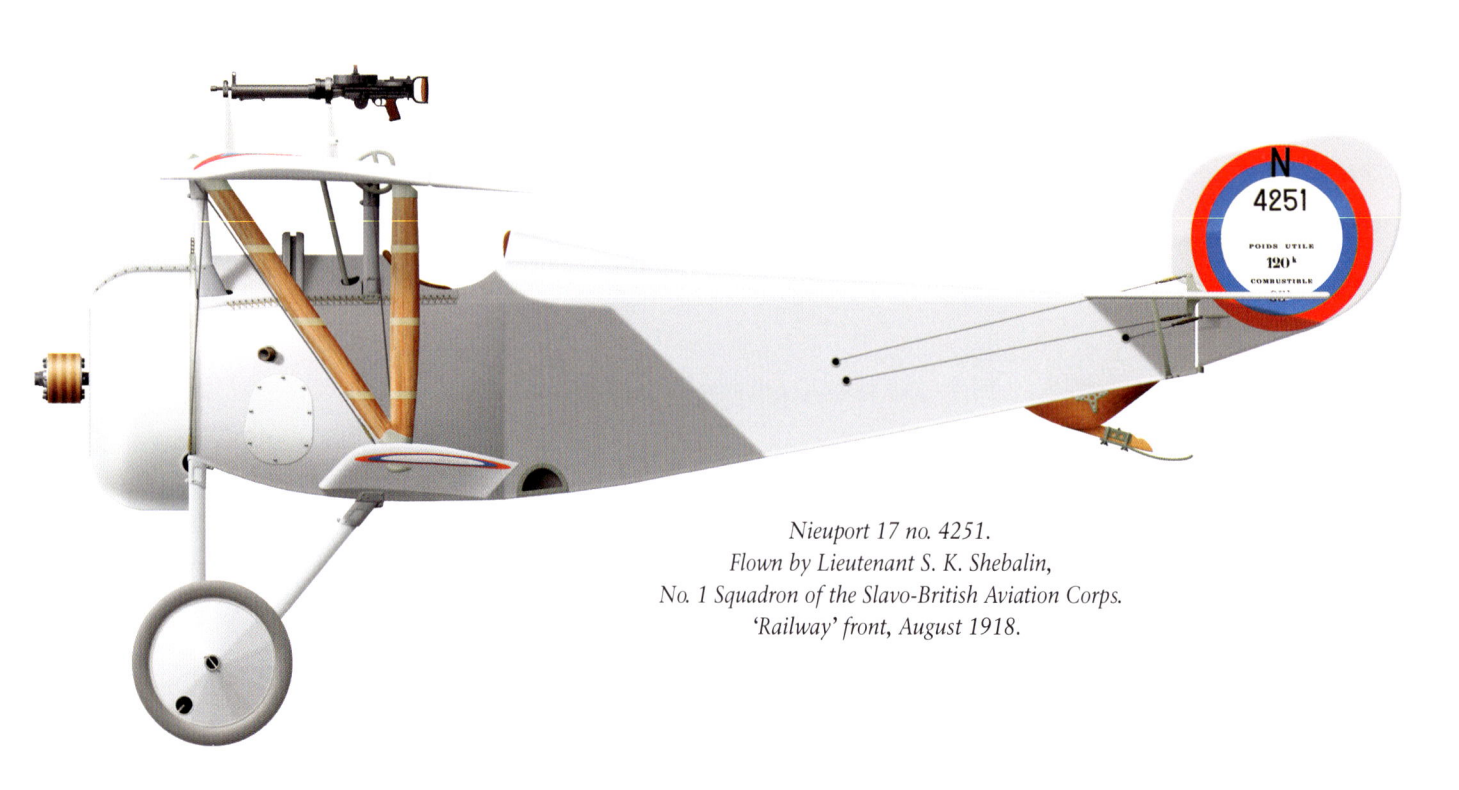

*Nieuport 17 no. 4251.
Flown by Lieutenant S. K. Shebalin,
No. 1 Squadron of the Slavo-British Aviation Corps.
'Railway' front, August 1918.*

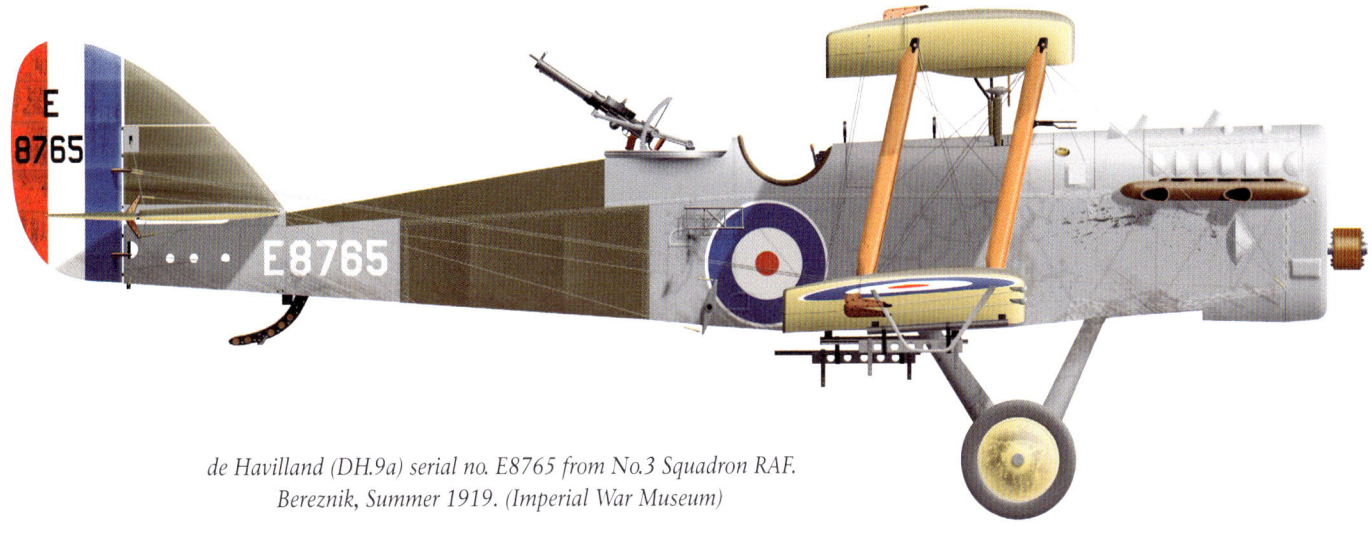

de Havilland (DH.9a) serial no. E8765 from No.3 Squadron RAF. Bereznik, Summer 1919. (Imperial War Museum)

Polkovnik A. A. Kozakov and kapitan S. K. Modrakh, a bit later kapitan Shebalin and Sveshnikov, received the rank of lieutenants in English service, the rest of the pilots were temporarily enlisted as airmen – with the stipulation of commission to officer ranks after the otryad was formed. By that time, shtabs-kapitan Slyusarenko, poruchik Kravets, pilot-aviator (civilian) Slyusarenko Sr. had arrived in Murman from Sweden, and podporuchik Baydak (managed to get through from Moscow), Tumanov, Tolstov and soldier-pilot Kropinov came from Arkhangel'sk. At the same time also podpolkovnik Barbas and kapitan Andreyev managed to make their way from Moscow.

Several engine mechanics could be found in Murman', where an English aviation otryad of Captain Robinson had soon arrived.

On 2 August (n.st.) Arkhangel'sk was occupied by allied, mostly British, troops and Captain Robinson's otryad moved there from Murmansk, as did all our pilots, joined in Arkhangel'sk by kapitan Belousovich, who had escaped from Moscow, and observer kornet Abramovich. In Arkhangel'sk polkovnik Kozakov began to form an aviation otryad, into which the observers, who until then served with local naval aviation, were accepted: podporuchik L'vovich and engineer brothers Derebizov.[42]

The otryad departed for the 'railway' front, to Obozerskaya station, in mid-August.

The 2nd Aviation Otryad SBAC (No. 2 Squadron SBAC) under *kapitan* Belousovich was sent, immediately after the formation, to the so-called 'river' front, where an airfield was prepared on the left bank of the Northern Dvina river near the village of Bereznik (Dvinskoy Bereznik), almost 300 versts from Arkhangel'sk. In mid-September they were joined by Kozakov's 1st Squadron.

---

42 Stat'ya "Na dal'nem Severe" ("In the Far North"), "Nasha Stikhiya" magazine. Simferopol'. No. 1 / August 1920. p. 9.

Snipe serial no. E6350, in which Major (British service). A. A. Kozakov crashed on 1 August 1919

Only the British were left on the 'railway' front.

Two Russian otryads actively fought on the 'river' and 'railway' fronts together with the British flights.[43]

By June 1919 a large number of aeroplanes had arrived in Arkhangel'sk, 21 de Havillands (DH.9) with Puma engines and 12 (DH.9A) with Liberty engines, 15 Snipes, six Avros and several R.E.8s. New British pilots also arrived. Now all the aviation forces in the North were split into four squadrons (No. 1 Squadron SBAC, No. 2, 3 and 4 Squadrons RAF). The first three squadrons were based at Bereznik, and the fourth at Obozerskaya. From among the newly arrived machines the Russian flyers (11 pilots and 11 observers) received four de Havillands and three Snipes, and the remaining Sopwiths were used for photography and spotting. The old Nieuport carried military mail, between Bereznik–front–

---

43 For more details on aviation activities in the North of Russia see V. Kulikov's article "Slavyano-britanskiy aviakorpus na Severe Rossii" ("Slavo-British Aviation Corps in the North of Russia"), published in the "AviaMaster" magazine, No. 1, 3/1999.

A drawing by K. K. Artseulov for the article "Aviatsiya na dal'nem Severe".
("Aviation in the Far North")
in the "Nasha Stikhiya" magazine, no. 1/1920.

A portrait of Captain (British service) A. A. Kozakov, published in the "Nasha Stikhiya" magazine. Bereznik, 28 May 1919.

Arkhangel'sk. The British noted the excellent work of Russian pilots. For example, in July alone the pilots of No. 1 Squadron SBAC accumulated 187 hours 47 minutes flying time and dropped 263 bombs with a total weight of 17,743 kg.

On 1 August *kapitans* Belousovich and Modrakh departed for Arkhangel'sk. *Mayor* Kozakov flew the Snipe, wishing to see his comrades-in-arms off, and also to test the recently overhauled machine. During a full right turn at an altitude of 100 meters his fighter went nose down and dived into the ground with its engine still running. Kozakov died on the spot, his spine broken …

He was replaced by *polkovnik* Shebalin as the commander of the Russian air unit. Combat operations did not continue for a long time, as in September No. 1 Squadron SBAC departed via England to the south of Russia, to Novorossiysk to continue the fight against the Reds. Upon arrival in Taganrog the 'Englishmen' were merged with the 4th Aviation Otryad of the AFSR, and Shebalin became its commander. Under Vrangel' in the Crimea, Shebalin's otryad was one of the best and was even mentioned in the orders of the Commander-in-Chief no. 3431 of 11 July 1920:

> In recognition of the military valour, courage and particularly brilliant work of the staff of the 4th Aviation Otryad displayed during combats from 25 May of this year, the otryad, in honour of the greatest Russian pilot, the hero polkovnik Kozakov, is to be called henceforth: "4th Aviation Otryad 'military pilot polkovnik Kozakov'".[44]

Murmansk Aviation Divizion

In May 1919 the British occupied the shore of Lake Onega in the north of the Bol'shaya guba bay, with the settlements of Povenets and Medvezh'ya Gora. To support the Onega flotilla, fifteen seaplanes (Fairey and Short) and ten land-based machines (Camel, R.E.8 and Avro) were delivered to Murmansk by the *Nairana*, *Pegasus* and *Argus* aircraft carriers.

For the Short and Fairey seaplanes of the so-called Forward Wing RAF Syren, a base was installed in the village of Medvezh'ya Gora, and for the land-based Camels (Aeroplane Unit Lumbushi) a place was chosen near the village of Lumbushi.

The first flights of the British took place in early June. They fought actively until almost the end of September, having flown a total of 616 hours and dropped 1,014 bombs weighing 28 tons during this time.[45]

---

44 RGVA. F. 40213. Op. 1. D. 1714. L. 415.
45 For details on the actions of the British on Onega see Phil Tomaselli's article "Faireys over lake Onega. Air operations with RAF Syren, Murmansk 1919" published in the "Cross & Cockade" magazine, Vol. 28, No. 3 of 1997

English Fairey IIID at Sortavala on 3 September 1919. From the cockade to the left English 1st Lieutenant Lingen-Kilburn and Captain Park, Captain Väinö Mikkola, 2nd Lieutenant Gunnar Appelgren, 1st Lieutenant Valto Salmi and 2nd Lieutenant Erland Nygrén. (K. Stenman coll.)

Fairey IIID serialled N9234 at Sortavala on 4 September 1919. The seaplane arrived on the previous day from a base located in the north-western part of Lake Onega. (K. Stenman coll.)

IIIC serial no. N9230 from the Forward Wing (RAF Syren). Flown by Captain W. H. Park. Medvezh'ya Gora, August 1919.

Fairey IIIC serial no. N9235 from the Nairana unit (RAF Syren). This machine flew the first combat sortie over Onega. Medvezh'ya Gora, June 1919.

Fairey IIIC serial no. N9239 from RAF Syren. Medvezh'ya Gora, Summer 1919.

Koivisto air station at the beginning of the 1920s. In turn, German, British and Finnish units were based here.
(K. Stenman coll.)

British aircraft mother ship HMS Vindictive *was based at the straits of Koivisto from July to November 1919.*
(K. Stenman coll.)

Camel serial no. F4055 from the Lumbushi Unit. In late August 1919 Lieutenant Sykes, due to an engine failure, was forced to land it at Petrozavodsk and was captured by the Reds.

A Grain Griffin belonging to HMS Vindictive *on a beach of the Gulf of Finland at Terijoki in summer 1919. A successful forced landing is here in question. (K. Stenman coll.)*

Short 184. An identical dual control seaplane was used by the British to train Russian pilots in the summer of 1919.

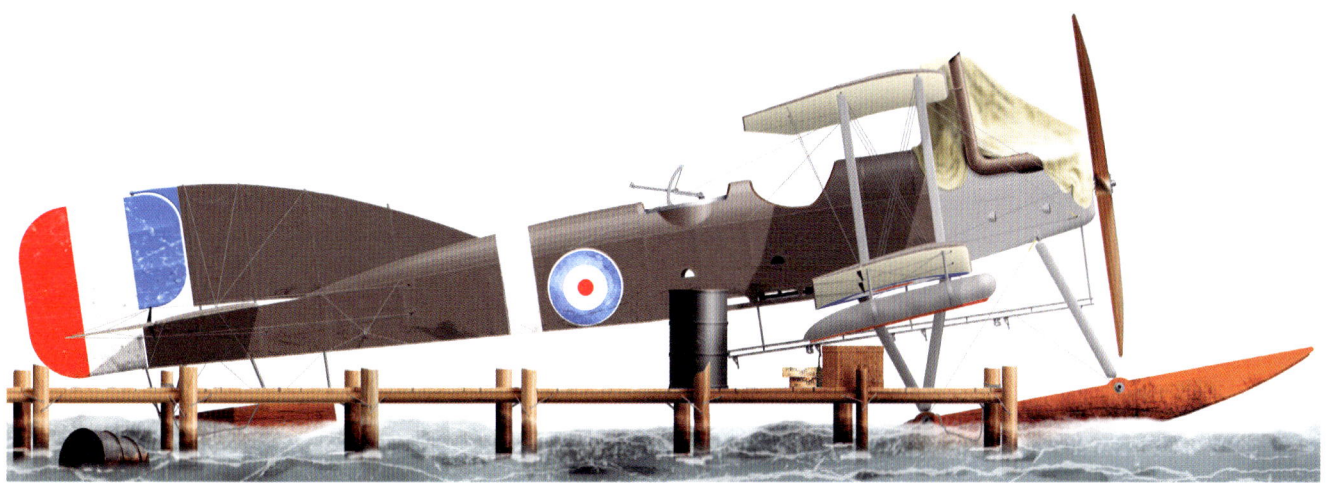

85

*Avro 504K serial no. E3708
flown on 6 October 1919 by praporshchik P. I. Anikin,
a pilot of the land-based Reconnaissance Otryad
of the Murmansk Aviation Divizion.*

*An Avro 504K captured in the north of Russia. Five-pointed red stars are visible on the lower wings, and the factory emblem on the fuselage.
(TsDAiK)*

SBAC airfield on Dvina. Avro 504K on the right, de Havillands on the left. 'River' front. Bereznik. Summer 1919

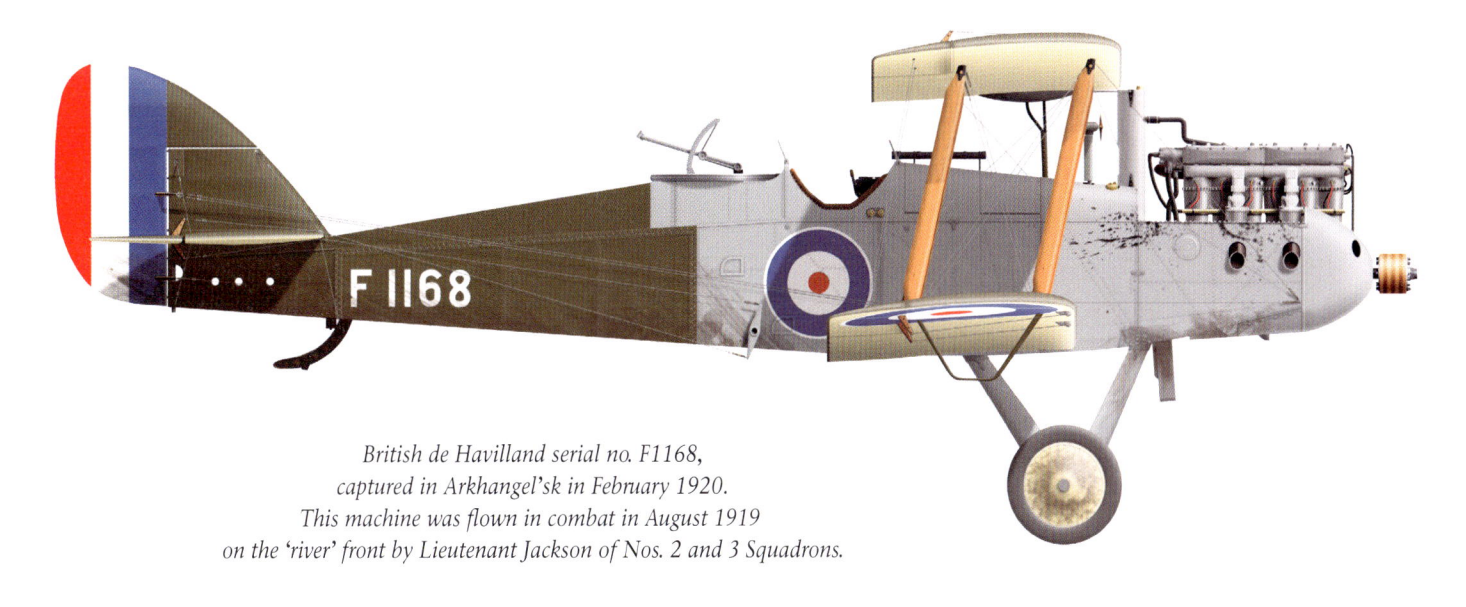

*British de Havilland serial no. F1168,
captured in Arkhangel'sk in February 1920.
This machine was flown in combat in August 1919
on the 'river' front by Lieutenant Jackson of Nos. 2 and 3 Squadrons.*

In July 1919 at Medvezh'ya Gora, Russian pilots started forming the Murmansk Aviation Division under military pilot *podpolkovnik* V. Z. Barbas. The White pilots trained flying the Short and Fairey seaplanes, and the Avro and Camel land-based biplanes. Two otryads were formed, the hydro-aviation one (commanded by *starshiy leytenant* I. S. Krayevskiy) and the land-based reconnaissance one (commanded by *poruchik* S. D. Gubin), to whom the British handed over their remaining machines, as they were leaving Russia in mid-September.

Altogether the division had 22 machines: three Grigorovich flying boats, three Shorts, two Faireys, three Camels, eight Avro-504Ks, one de Havilland, one Sopwith 1½-Strutter and one R.E.8. Notably, there were many more aeroplanes than pilots. All orders for the divizion have survived, but they do not include a single word about recognition markings. This fact, along with numerous photos of captured British aeroplanes, once again confirms that the British markings remained unaltered on the machines transferred to the Russians.

1ˢᵗ Aviation Otryad of the Northern Front

> Orders
> Commander-in-Chief of all Russian Forces on the Northern Front
>
> No. 309
>
> 5 October 1919 Arkhangel'sk
>
> §14.
>
> I order to immediately start forming aviation units of the Northern Front: the Aviation Otryad and the Aviation Base. The designated units as independent units must begin to operate only after the completion of all work, both above named units should be seen as the aviation detachment of the 1ˢᵗ Automobile Divizion, whose Commander should provide the necessary assistance to facilitate the work, both during forming and the continuous one, to support flights.
>
> General surveillance of the work on the forming of the otryad and the base, and the putting of the property in order is entrusted to the General-Quartermaster.
>
> *Signed: General Staff, General-leytenant Miller**
>
> * *RGVA. F. 39450. Op. 1. D. 201. L. 397.*

The aviation otryad formed in Arkhangel'sk at the Automobile Divizion of *polkovnik* Korotkevich received the name 1ˢᵗ Aviation Otryad of the Northern Front. The otryad was commanded by military pilot *poruchik* Tumanov, and the establishment pilot posts were held by *leytenant* Yakovitskiy and *starshiy unter-ofitsers* Vershinskiy and Dushutin. By early November the otryad had been formed, and two Snipes with British recognition markings (pilots Tumanov and Yakovitskiy) were despatched to the front line, to Obozerskaya station. In November-December 1919 pilots of the 1ˢᵗ Aviation Otryad managed to fly several reconnaissance and bombing sorties. In February 1920 Red Army troops occupied Arkhangel'sk, and in March Murmansk was captured. The Northern Front of the White Forces ceased to exist. In early March 1920 a report was sent from Arkhangel'sk to Moscow about the war prizes:

> *six aeroplanes of serviceable systems: de Havilland (250 hp engines) – two, Avro with 130 hp Clerget – one, Snipe with 250 hp B.R. – two, Camel with 120 hp Rhône – one, unserviceable: de Havilland – one, [...] six warm hangars for 18 aeroplanes, workshops and depots, [...].*[46]

One of the prizes was *leytenant* Yakovitskiy's Snipe with the name "Nelly" on its side, in which the Red military pilot Sapozhnikov subsequently fought and died.[47]

Arkhangel'sk airfield. A captured Avro and de Havilland can be seen among the aeroplanes of the 2ⁿᵈ Reconnaissance Aviation Otryad RKKVVF. February 1920. (TsDAiK)

---

46 RGVA. F. 188. Op. 3. D. 223. L. 100.
47 Sapozhnikov's aeroplane is presented in Chapter 5 on pages 26 and 61.

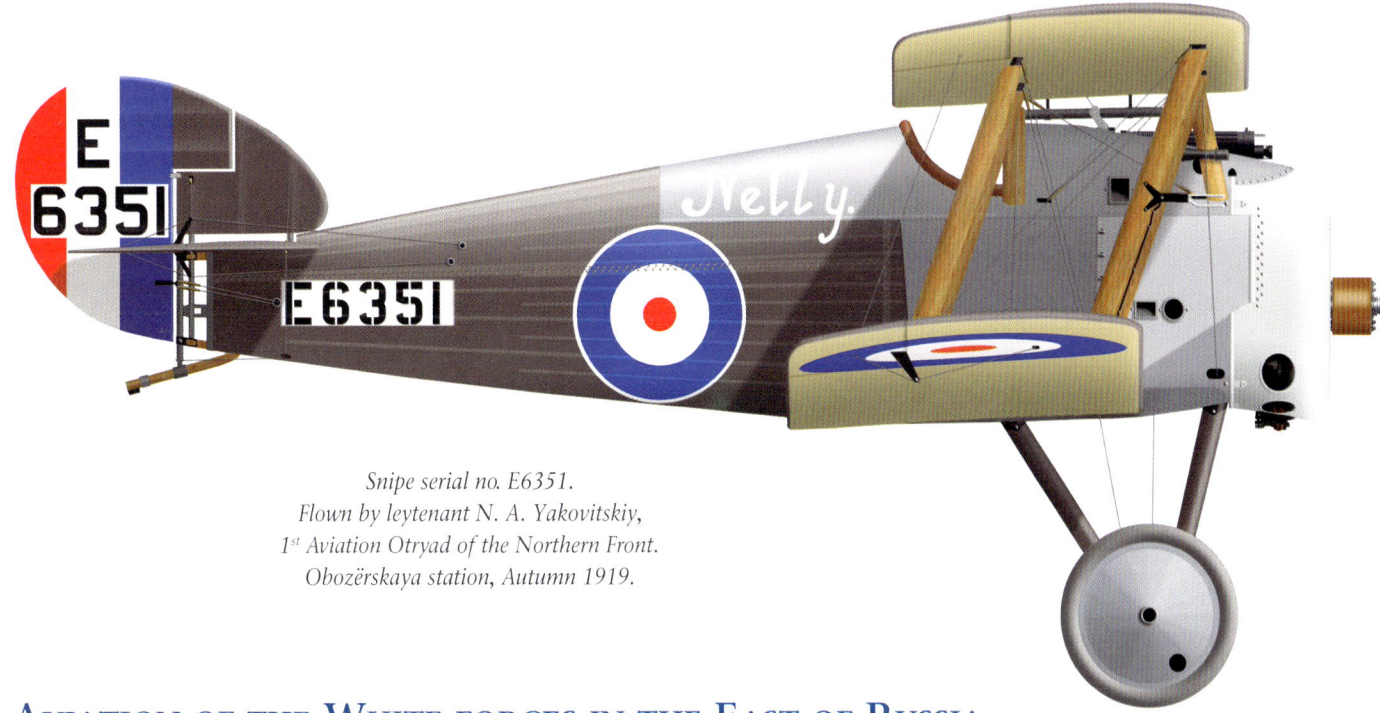

*Snipe serial no. E6351.
Flown by leytenant N. A. Yakovitskiy,
1st Aviation Otryad of the Northern Front.
Obozërskaya station, Autumn 1919.*

Aviation of the White forces in the East of Russia

People's Army

On 8 June 1918 Samara was captured by troops of the Czechoslovak Corps, which had started to mutiny in connection with the intention of the Soviet government to disarm and intern them. The mutiny of 'the White Czechs' (Czecho-Slovak Corps) created opportunities for the organisation of the first anti-Bolshevik government in Samara (*Komuch – Komitet chlenov Vserossiyskogo uchreditel'nogo sobraniya*, Committee of Members of the All-Russian Constituent Assembly), which claimed all-Russian status.

By the first orders of the Komuch the General Staff the formation of the Volunteer People's Army in the territory controlled by the government, as well as for the organisation of law enforcement in the city and the province, was organised. *Polkovnik* N. A. Galkin was appointed the Chief of Staff and the Commander of the People's Army.

At that time the following were based in the province, the former Bolshevik 1st Samara Aviation Otryad and the HQ of the 1st Aviation Divizion in Samara, the 5th Corps' Aviation Otryad in Syzran'. On 21 June 1918 these units were renamed as the 1st, 2nd and 3rd Aviation Otryads and included in the People's Army. On 15 July the 33rd Corps' Aviation Otryad (4th Aviation Otryad) also joined the army.

The story of the People's Army aviation would be incomplete without a brief history of the Czechoslovak aviation otryad.

The so-called 1st Czecho-Slovak Aviation and Automobile Detachment was formed in late February/early March 1918. The detachment received nine aircraft (from the aviation park in Kiev, from the French air mission in Kiev). On the basis of an agreement with the Soviet authorities on disarmament, at the end of March the machines had to be given up, and upon arrival in Vladivostok in June 1918 the unit was disbanded. One of the organisers of the detachment, *podporučík* Melč, stayed behind in Samara for family reasons and after the mutiny of his compatriots in the Volga region he became the initiator of the creation of a new air unit of the Czech forces. Thus, on the basis of the 1st Samara Aviation Otryad, which had moved to the side of the People's Army after the fall of Samara, Melč organised a combat platoon, having taken the first Farman 30 from the otryad.

Russian pilots and observers also served with the detachment. On 31 August 1918, by order no. 44 of the People's Army, the Combat Platoon of the 1st Aviation Otryad was renamed "Independent[48] Aviation Otryad at the 1st Czecho-Slovak Hussite Rifle Division."[49] In 1918 'Czechoslovak' aeroplanes carried traditional Russian recognition markings, as evidenced by surviving photographs.

From 11 September 1918 the Czech Aviation Otryad was equipped with a Nieuport 21 fighter, no. 1940, flown in by the commander of the 23rd Corps' Air Squadron, Red pilot Gusev. He alighted near Cherdakly station, and the next day his aeroplane was ferried to the location of the Special Aviation Otryad, to Kindyakovka station, by pilot Dedyulin. In 1919, when the Czech detachment was in Omsk, photos show that the aeroplane plane was still carrying Russian three-colour roundels.

---

48 In all documents the first word in the name of the detachment was "Osobyy" ("Special"), rather than "Otdel'nyy" ("Independent").
49 RGVA. F. 39551. Op. 1. D. 16. L. 64.

Nieuport 21 no. 1873, armed with an over-wing Hotchkiss machine gun. The machine was in service with the 5th Corps' Aviation Otryad from April 1917, flown by praporshchik K. N. Speranskiy, who continued to fly it in the People's Army until February 1919. (TsDAiK)

Farman 30 biplane. The 33rd Corps' Aviation Otryad. The shoulder strap insignia of a 'military pilot' is painted on the roundel in Russian national colours. The eagle has no crown. Autumn 1918.

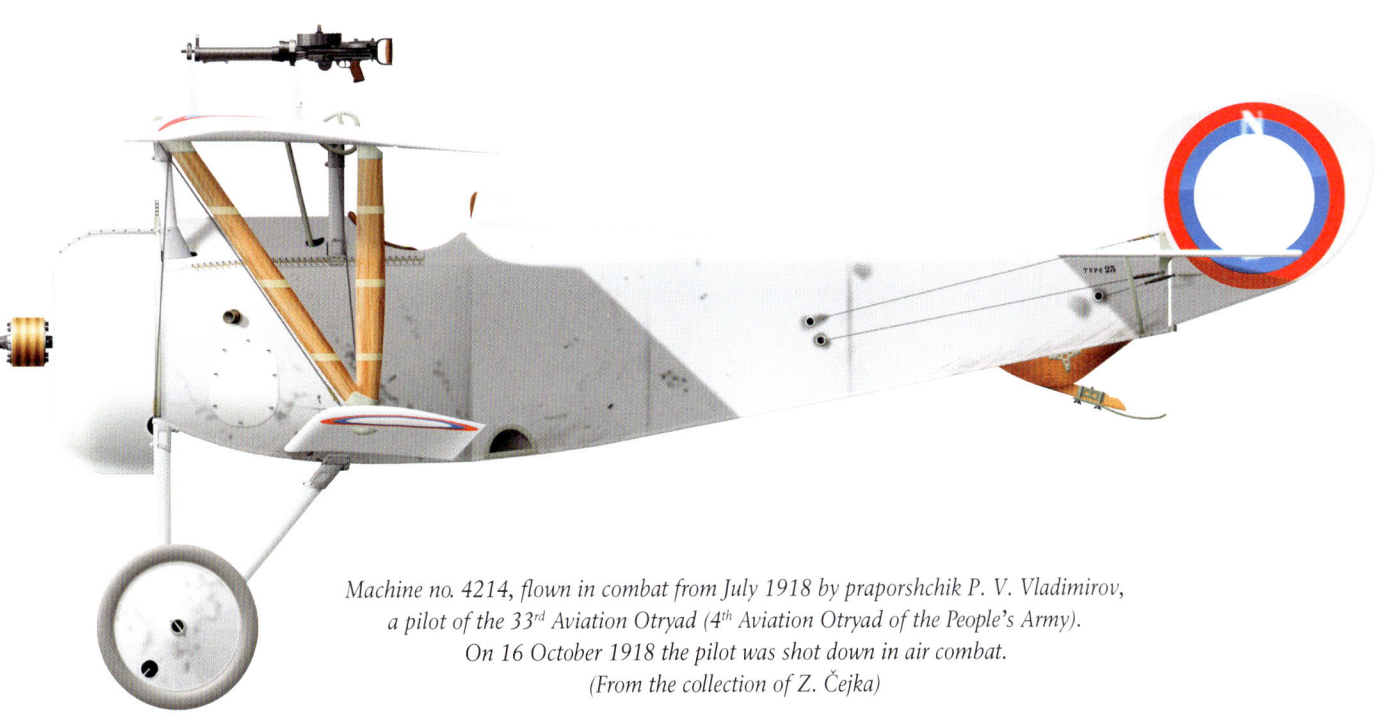

*Machine no. 4214, flown in combat from July 1918 by praporshchik P. V. Vladimirov,
a pilot of the 33rd Aviation Otryad (4th Aviation Otryad of the People's Army).
On 16 October 1918 the pilot was shot down in air combat.
(From the collection of Z. Čejka)*

*French production
Nieuport 17 fighter
no. 4214.
From September 1917
the machine was used
by the 33rd Corps' Aviation
Otryad. Flown
by praporshchik
P. F. Kachan.
Northern Front.
Autumn 1917.
(From the collection
of V. P. Kulikov)*

*Duks built Farman 30 no. 1737. Flown by podporučík L. Melč, combat platoon of the 1st Samara Aviation Otryad of the People's Army. The machine was downed while with the 33rd Corps' Aviation Otryad (4th Aviation Otryad of the People's Army).
Ufa, July 1918.
(From the collection of Z. Čejka)*

*A train of the Special Aviation Otryad at the 1st Czech-Slovak Hussite Rifle Division. Duks-built aeroplanes are seen here, Nieuport 21 no. 1359 and Farman 30 no. 1695.
Miass station, November 1918.
(From the collection of Z. Čejka)*

Duks built Nieuport 21 no. 1940. Flown by praporshchik A. G. Dedyulin. Aviation otryad of the Czechoslovak forces. Omsk, May–June 1919. (From the collection of Z. Čejka)

On 7 August 1918, after persistent battles, Kazan' was occupied by the White forces. The following aviation units of the Bolsheviks fell into the hands of the People's Army: the 6th Aviation Park, the Petrograd Aviation School, the transport train of the Gatchina Military Aviation School. The personnel and aeroplanes were used when forming the 2nd Aviation Group of the People's Army, which consisted of four otryads (5th, 6th, 7th and 8th).

Almost immediately, orders were issued on the new recognition markings of the People's Army aeroplanes.

**Orders no. 2
of the Authority of the Air Force at the Staff of the People's Army.**

15 August 1918 Kazan'

§1.
I appoint the Head of the Petrograd Aviation School, military pilot *shtabs-kapitan* Rybakov, as the Commander of the 2nd Aviation Group.

§2.
I announce for information and execution that the RECOGNITION MARKINGS on all combat aircraft of the People's Army should be as follows:
Roundels of national colours and longitudinal stripes of St George colours on the lower surface.

*Head of the Air Force at the Staff of the People's Army, Military engineer, military pilot, kapitan Boreyko**

* RGVA. F. 39499. Op. 1. D. 295. L. 2.

This document was preceded by orders to the troops of the People's Army no. 20 issued earlier (on 25 July), known to historians, which detailed the external appearance and rules for wearing a new uniform and insignia for the troops of the People's Army. In Appendix no. 1 to Orders no. 20 "Description of the uniform of the servicemen of the People's Army", in para. "v", in particular, it was established that

> *the headgear is a camouflage colour forage cap, temporarily, until the establishment of the cockade, with the* **St George ribbon** *on the band diagonally (from right to left).*[50]

White aviators in Kazan' opposed the aviation of the 5th Red Army, operating from the airfield near Sviyazhsk station.[51] There were very few aerial engagements. Here is one of the reports of the Reds about a meeting with the enemy, in which the markings of the People's Army aeroplanes are mentioned.

Report of the Chief of Staff of the Air Force of the 5th Army, no. 51.

Today [20 August] at 6.10 a Lebed' type enemy aeroplane was spotted above the airfield at an altitude of 250-300 metres. It has appeared from the railway station side. The recognition markings it had were as follows: **St George ribbon around the fuselage.**

Moreover, at an altitude of 1,800 meters another enemy machine of the Parasol type [was spotted] and even higher a Nieuport fighter, apparently Type 23, as it proved to be very fast.

In addition to these three machines pilots subsequently saw a fighter of the Nieuport type.

For the pursuit, three of our fighter aircraft of the 1st Soviet Combat Aviation Group were scrambled: Commander of the group military pilot Pavlov and pilots Ingaunis and Bakin.

Military pilot Pavlov took off about three minutes after the 1st enemy aircraft was spotted. He chased the enemy Nieuport fighter, which he attacked several times beyond Sviyazhsk.

The enemy aeroplane began to escape Pavlov in a descent, but comrade Pavlov pursued him, descending down to 300 metres over the river Volga.

The remaining enemy aircraft also escaped back after our pilots took off.

Chief of staff of the Air Force, military pilot Akashev.
Secretary, pilot-observer Grigor'ev*

* *RGVA. F. 185. Op. 3. D. 953. L. 17.*

Aeroplanes of the White unit suffered more from friendly ground fire than from the action of Red fighters. That was why a document was issued that discussed again the markings of the aviation of the People's Army.

Orders no. 12
to the troops of the Northern Group and to the garrison of Kazan' city
29 August 1918

On 28 August our best aeroplane was shot down in the city by fire of our own anti-aircraft batteries and indiscriminate machine-gun and rifle fire of infantry units. The machine had clearly visible identification markings – **St George ribbons.**

In order to avoid similar sad cases in the future, I order:

1) all anti-aircraft platoons, as well as all guns that can fire on aerial machines, contact immediately the Aviation Staff and the Head of all aviation otryads, without whose permission no single gun is allowed to open fire.

[…]

Commander of the Northern Group Forces polkovnik Stepanov.
Chief of Staff general-leytenant Romanovskiy*

* *"Narodnaya zhizn'" newspaper, No. 8 of 1 September 1918, Kazan'.*

---

50   RGVA. F. 39551. Op. 1. D. 16. L. 64.
51   See Chapter 5 for information about the 1st Soviet Combat Aviation Group, which fought at Kazan'.

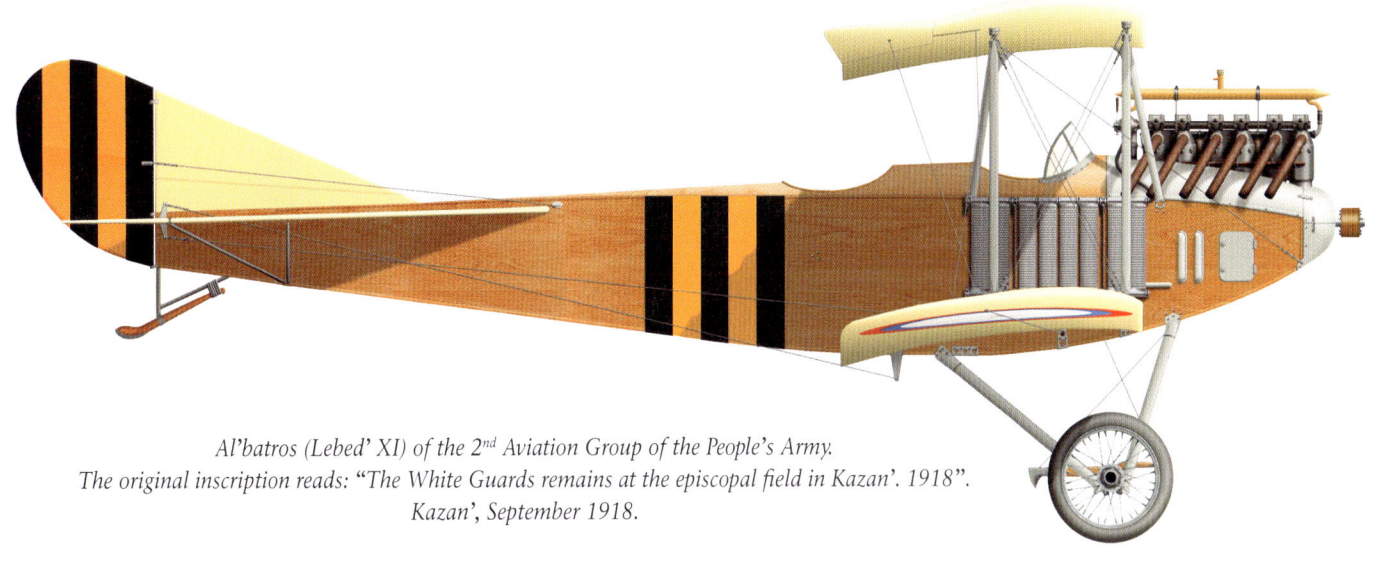

Al'batros (Lebed' XI) of the 2nd Aviation Group of the People's Army.
The original inscription reads: "The White Guards remains at the episcopal field in Kazan'. 1918".
Kazan', September 1918.

So far only one photo is known where the St George ribbons are visible on the aeroplane. Aviators of the Reds pose against the backdrop of a People's Army machine that crashed into a forest. Ribbons of St George flowers are painted on the rudder and on the side of the remains of the Lebed' 12.

Another picture, taken after the capture of Kazan', shows an aeroplane of the People's Army, which had suffered an accident. The machine has retained the Russian three-colour roundels.

Concluding the story about the aviation of the People's Army, it is also necessary to mention that it included for a short time the 9th Ural and 1st (10th numbered) Orenburg Aviation Otryads.[52]

---

[52] For more details on the history of these aviation units, see V. Peshkov, M. Khairulin. "Aviatsionnyye formirovaniya Ural'skoy Armii 1918–1919 gg." ("Aviation formations of the Ural Army 1918–1919") p. 54–112, "Gorynych"" almanac, part 1/2007; A. Ganin, M. Khairulin. "Nablyudatel' vyskochil na krylo… Aviatsionnyye formirovaniya Yuzhnogo Urala 1918–1919 gg." ("The observer has jumped out onto the wing… Aviation formations of the Southern Ural 1918–1919"), "Rodina" magazine No. 9/2007, pp. 74–79.

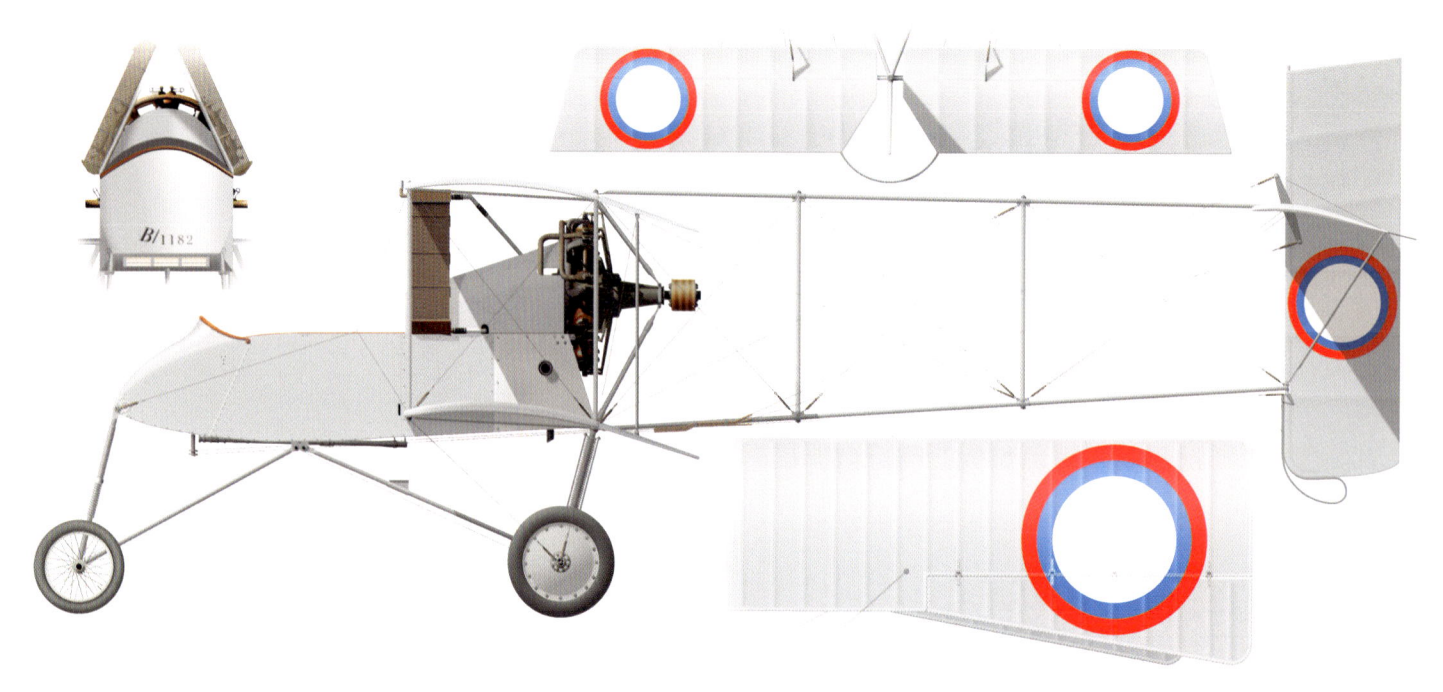

Voisin no. B/1182 of the 2nd Aviation Group of the People's Army, which suffered an accident at the Kazan' airfield and was abandoned during the retreat by the White troops. Kazan', September 1918. (TsDAiK)

Some information was found about the recognition markings of Cossack aeroplanes.

> **Announcement for residents of the city of Ural'sk**
>
> 1) During flights of enemy aeroplanes over Ural'sk there will be frequent prolonged ringing at fireboxes,
>
> 2) it is forbidden to fire at enemy aeroplanes;
>
> 3) distinctive markings of Cossack aeroplanes – **two black crossed stripes for the entire length of each wing and rudder.**
>
> *Quartermaster General of the Ural Army*
> *general-mayor Palenov**
>
> * *"Yaitskaya Volya" newspaper No. 10 of 3/16 January 1919, Ural'sk*

Orenburg aeroplanes, it seems, displayed standard Russian First World War roundels.

The armed forces of the All-Russian Government (admiral A. V. Kolchak's)

Simultaneously with the creation of the aviation of the People's Army, aviation units were being formed in Siberia from June 1918. Thus, by mid-July, the 1st and 2nd Siberian Aviation Otryads of the West Siberian Army were formed. Soon they were joined by the Bolshevik Orenburg Aviation Otryad, which had defected to the White side in July, and was renamed the 3rd Siberian Otryad. From August 1918 the army began to be called Siberian and it now included three complete aviation otryads.

A train of the 1st Siberian Aviation Otryad before departure to the front line. Otryad staff posing with two Duks-built Farman 30s. Caps as well as sleeves of some of the Siberian aviators are adorned with white-green ribbons and black shields (shoulder patch markings). (From the collection of Z. Čejka)

On 23 September 1918 the Ufa Directory ("Provisional All-Russian Government") was established and on 9 October moved from Ufa to Omsk. It was recognised by all regional, national and Cossack governments, the Siberian regional duma, the provisional Siberian government and the Komuch.

When the troops of the People's Army retreated from the Volga to Siberia, in October the Samara and Kazan' aviation units merged into one under the command of the Authority of the Air Force at the Staff of the Supreme Commander-in-Chief (commanded by military pilot *kapitan* D. A. Boreyko).[53] From that time on, the Siberian otryads also began to report to that HQ. Thus, by November 1918, the combined troops, subordinate to the Directory, had thirteen aviation otryads.

---

53 Until 8 October 1918: Authority of the Air Force at the Staff of the People's Army.

After the Omsk coup, on 18 November 1918, admiral A. V. Kolchak became the Supreme Commander-in-Chief of all land and naval forces of Russia (replacing *general-leytenant* V. G. Boldyrev) and the Supreme Ruler.

Assembly of a Voisin at an airfield of the 3rd Aviation Otryad (5th Corps' Aviation Otryad). Lebed' 12 no. 585 is in the makeshift hangar. The Russian three-colour roundel can be seen on its fuselage. South-Western Front, Kartaly station (near Orenburg) Winter 1918/1919. (From the collection of Z. Čejka)

The 1st Siberian Corps' Aviation Otryad (originally the Aviation Otryad of the Primor'ye Region Forces) was formed at the air school at Spasskoye village in Primor'ye, from September 1918. In February 1919 the unit was disbanded and two Siberian Aviation Otryads were formed on its basis, numbered the 14th and 15th. This was because, in December 1918, Boreyko issued orders according to which the 1st, 2nd and 3rd Siberian Aviation Otryads were re-numbered the 11th, 12th and 13th, respectively. Only after a request by the Siberian aviators in February 1919 did the units resumed their former names.

Hydro-aviation also existed in Kolchak's Siberia. Due to a number of circumstances, naval pilots who had previously served in the Baltic with four flying boats and a number of aero engines arrived in Krasnoyarsk in 1918. This allowed the formation the Krasnoyarsk hydro-aviation station, which provided the basis for a combat otryad under naval pilot *starshiy leytenant* V. M. Marchenko for operations on the Kama. A barge was equipped in Perm' for the 1st Hydro-Otryad. The detachment also received two M-9 machines, which were captured on 14 May at Yelabuga.

> *The Hydroplanes were sent to Perm' city for inspection and to bring them back into order", recalled kontr-admiral M. I. Smirnov. "Our pilots tried to fly them, but could not stay airborne for more than 20 minutes. It turned out that the engines were extremely soiled, because instead of petrol the Bolsheviks had used a mixture of alcohol and ether – obviously they did not have petrol. The engines were cleaned, and the aircraft soon began to fly combat sorties.*

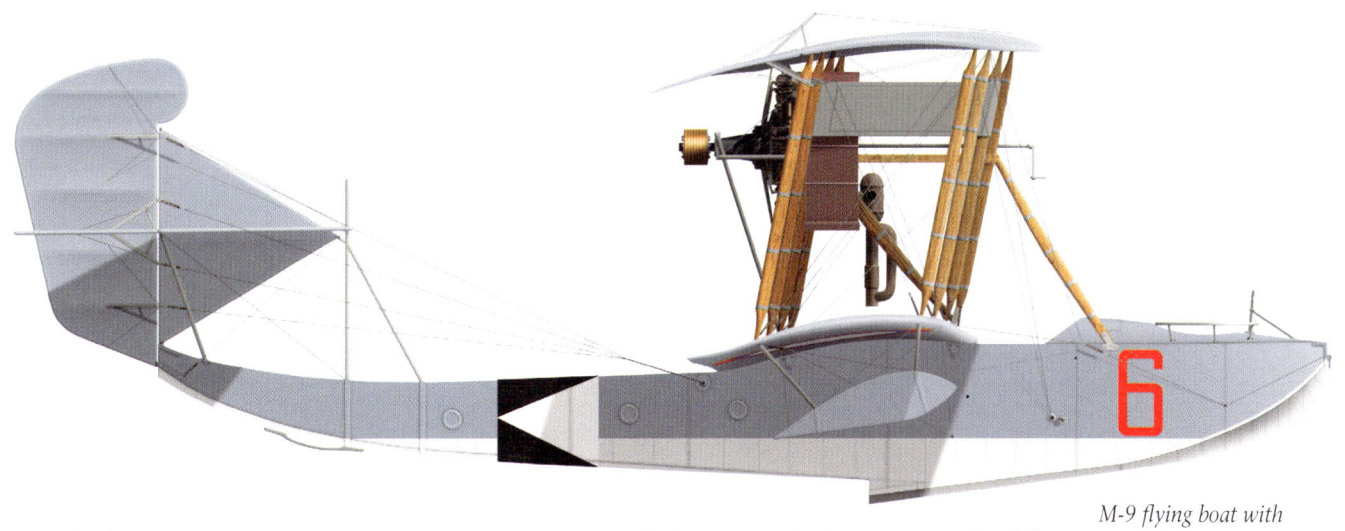

M-9 flying boat with otryad no. 6. 1919. (From the collection of G. F. Petrov)

A similar white triangle (pennant) is present on the fuselage of the machine taking off. No otryad no. on the fuselage is visible, but there are Russian roundels on the upper wings. 1919. (TsVMM)

99

In June the naval aviators fought alongside the Kama River Combat Flotilla.[54]

Several photographs of Kolchak's machines survive. A strange marking was applied on the fuselages of the hydroplanes, white triangles on a black band, dark circles on light and white ones on black background, and also two black and one white bands. Presumably, black and white colours were used for these markings. Russian three-colour circles were applied on upper and lower wings and the rudders displayed the Russian flag colours, white-blue-red. Code numbers in the range of 1 to 6 applied on fuselage sides are also known.

This and opposite page: M-9 flying boats on a barge of the 1st Hydro-Aviation otryad. Kama. Two variants of marking are visible, a white disc on a black background and a black disc on white. Summer 1919. (TsVMM)

---

54 Aleksandrov A. O. "Pobedy. Poteri… Zadachi, podrazdeleniya, nachal'stvuyushchiy sostav, letatel'nyye apparaty i vooruzheniye morskoy aviatsii i vozdukhoplavaniya Rossii, a takzhe spisok pobed i poter's 1894-go po 1920 g." ("Victories, losses… Tasks, units, commanding staff, aircraft and armament of the naval aviation and aeronautics of Russia, and the listing of victories and losses 1894–1920") – SPb.: "IP Kompleks", 2000. p. 58, 62.

101

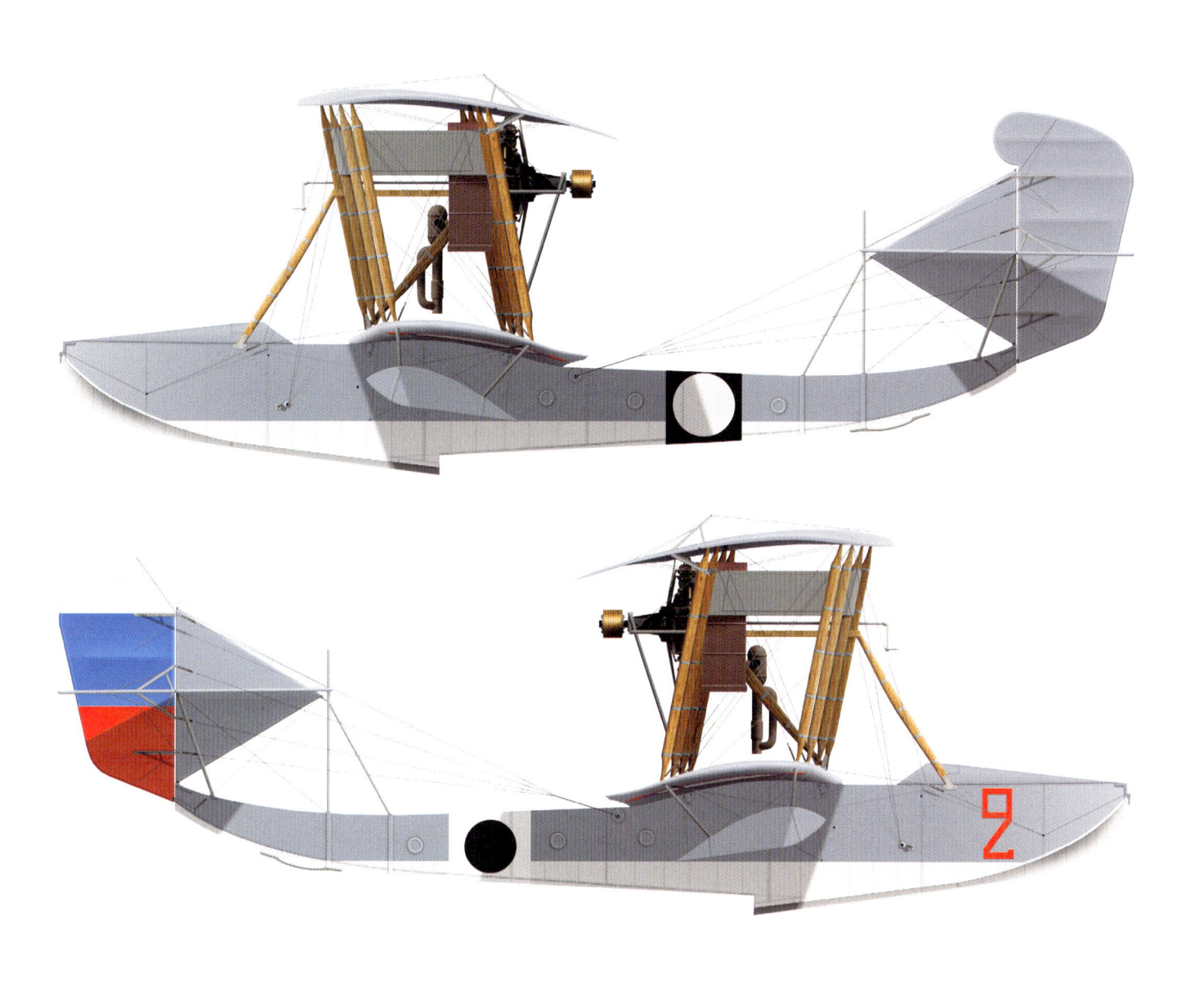

The flying hydroplane displays a noticeable marking in the form of a black disc on a white band, as well as three-colour roundels on the lower wings. (TsVMM)

102

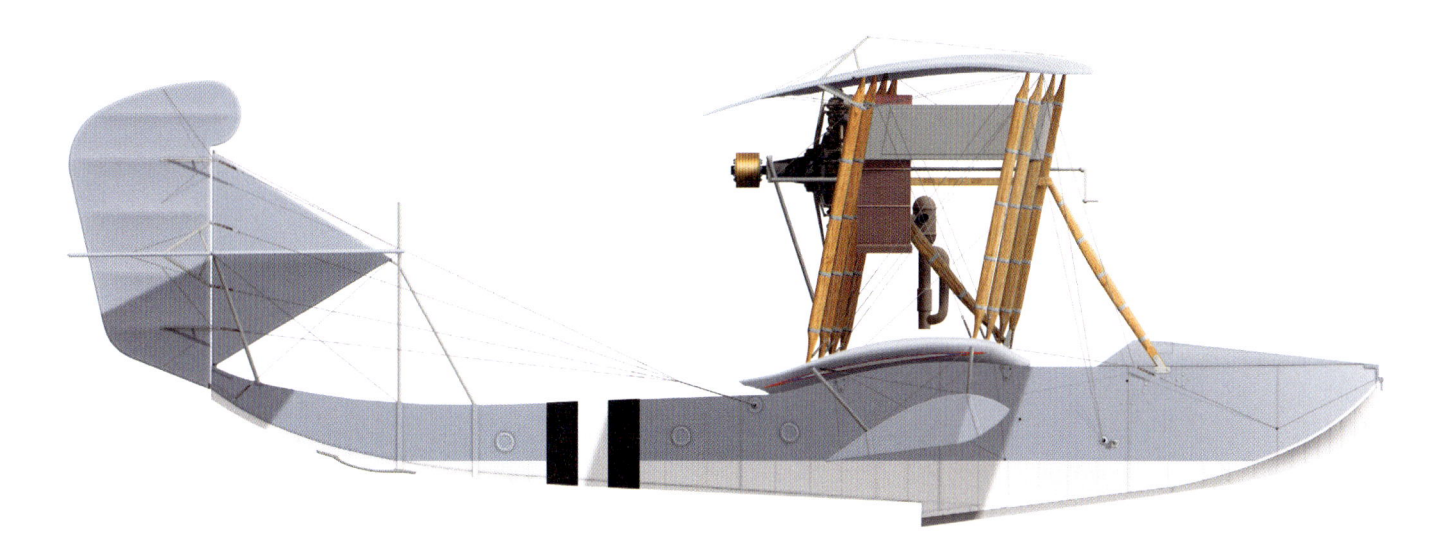

A marking in the form of two dark and one light bands is noticeable on the hydroplane hull undergoing an overhaul. (TsVMM)

'Let us get back to land-based aviation. Throughout the campaign of 1919, Kolchak's aeroplanes flew with Russian three-colour roundels. This is confirmed by a number of photos. It is possible that some machines continued to fly with St George ribbons. Intelligence data obtained in the summer of 1919 pointed out that "*the recognition markings of the machines: St George ribbon on the tail, roundels overpainted…*" But it seems this was an exception to the rules, or the data was obsolete.

The report of *kapitan* Belov, the head of the Air Force of the Siberian Army, dated 28 June 1919, shows how dilapidated and old the aeroplanes of the land-based aviation otryads were:

> *Today I returned from a trip to Perm' to inspect the aviation units. I inspected the 2nd Siberian Aviation Otryad and the 1st echelon of the 3rd Siberian Aviation Otryad, heading from Osa to Kungur, the combat part of which is currently located on the Talaya river, to the south of Osa. When inspecting the aeroplanes of the 2nd Siberian Aviation Otryad it turned out that there were three present: one Farman and two Sopwiths, one of which had flown over from the Reds in March. All the machines are so dilapidated and have a large number of operational flights. On the Farman 30 the main planes, due to lack of enamel, are covered with a simple white oil paint (oil paint does not have the property of the enamel to shrink the canvas, which for this reason dangles like a stretched sail, in flight all this risks being torn off). The Sopwith – "red", as it is called in the otryad – is still relatively fit for combat work. Another Sopwith, due to frequent breakages, does not represent particular value. The fourth, a Voisin, was crashed by pilots and is now in the workshop. The combat machines are brought to unserviceability even quicker by the absence of tents…*[55]

---

55   RGVA. F. 40025. Op. 1. D. 18. L. 12.

*French production
Morane-Parasol trainer.
Military Aviation School
of the Far East,
Spasskoye village
1919 or 1920.
(From the family archive
of S. V. Kharchev)*

*French production
Nieuport 23 no. 4279.
Flown by praporshchik
A. D. Muratov,
3rd Siberian Aviation
Otryad. The markings
and stencilling
on the aeroplane are still
in the form in which
it was delivered from
France to Russia in 1917.
Summer 1919.
(From the family archive
of Tikhomirov)*

Siberian aviation workshops of engineer M. I. Popov were located in the town of Novo-Nikolayevsk. In addition to manufacturing aeroplanes of his own design, in the summer of 1918 the talented engineer organised overhauls and assembly of machines for the Siberian Army's aviation otryads. For example, the remains of Vladimirov's aeroplane and of a crashed Nieuport 23 sent in by the 33rd Aviation Otryad in December 1918 were used in the workshops to assemble the Popov VII single-seat fighter.

The work was financed by the Novo-Nikolayevsk Stock Exchange Committee, who modestly reminded themselves by sending a telegram to the Minister of War:

> *While rejoicing at the opportunity to help our army, we send our greetings and, as a gift, the fighter aeroplane, built in Novo-Nikolayevsk by engineer Popov with the resources of the stock exchange committee. May God help save Russia and its peoples from the troubles that are being experienced.*[56]

At the end of September 1919 the Popov VII fighter (without engine) was ceremonially handed over to the 3rd Siberian Aviation Otryad. The machine featured an inscription on the wings:

> *A gift of the Novo-Nikolayevsk Stock Exchange Committee to the valiant Third SibAviaOtryad.*[57]

---

[56] "Tsennyy podarok" ("Valuable gift"), "Sibirskiy kazak" newspaper No. 1 of 10 September 1919, Omsk. p. 3.
[57] RGVA. F. 39499. Op. 1. D. 316. L. 36.

In October *praporshchik* Snegirëv managed to perform only two test flights in this machine. During 1920–1921 'Popov's seven' was used by one of the aviation otryads of the People's Revolutionary Army of the Far Eastern Republic and, it can be presumed, without the presentation inscription on the wings.

Let us return to the 'Czechoslovak aviation'. As early as December 1918, 25 American LWF model V aeroplanes were delivered to Vladivostok for the Czech legionnaires, and these became known in Russia under the name of 'Sturtevant' after the name of the engine. According to the orders of General Janin, the Head of the French military mission in Siberia, and also thanks to the efforts of the Kolchak aviation HQ, 18 machines were purchased from Czechoslovaks (at US$13,000 per aeroplane).

The remaining seven 'Americans' arrived in Omsk in late May with the Czechoslovak airmen, and there they joined the former "Special Aviation Otryad at the 1st Czecho-Slovak Hussite Rifle

Czechoslovak Nieuport 21 and LWFs (nos. 39930 and 39953) in a hangar. Omsk, Summer 1919. (From the collection of Z. Čejka)

Nieuport 21 and some LWFs in Nikol'sko-Ussuriysk. All machines display the red-white rudders and American recognition markings. Autumn 1919. (From the collection of Z. Čejka)

A Czechoslovak LWF, code no. 7. Omsk. Summer 1919.

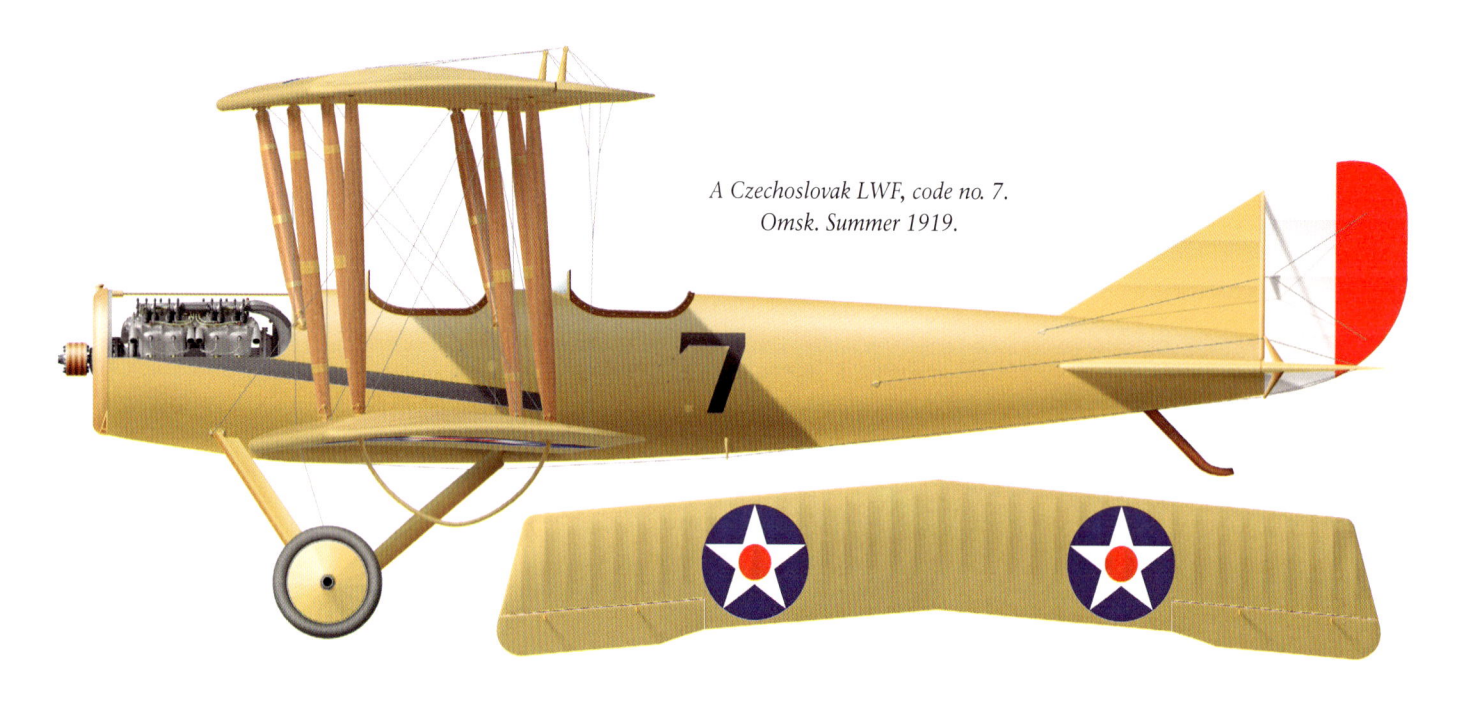

LWF model V biplane on display at the Národní Technické Muzeum in Prague. (NTM/Praha)

Division", which had been there since March with two Nieuport 21s and one Farman 30. An aviation school was organised in Omsk. The otryad was now reporting directly to the HQ of the Czechoslovak Forces in Russia and received the name "Aviation Otryad of the Czech Forces". The flying school in Omsk operated until early August, and then moved to Nikol'sk-Ussuriyskiy. And finally, on 10 January 1920, the Czechoslovaks loaded their aeroplanes onto a ship in Vladivostok (the Nieuports and Farman remained in Russia) and sailed home. One of the 'Americans' has survived to this day and is an exhibit of the Národní Technické Muzeum (National Technical Museum) in Prague.

LWF code no. 68.

The first photo (code no. 83) was taken in the United States. The other one in Russia (code no. 78, among others). (From the collection of Z. Čejka)

The airfield of the Kurgan Military Aviation School. The photo shows two LWFs: one with code no. 58 or 68, the other has American recognition markings on the upper wings. Kurgan, Summer 1919. (From the family archive of M. F. Ivkov)

LWF biplane. Three-colour roundels are applied on the lower wing and three-colour stripes on the rudder. Military Aviation School of the Far East, Spasskoye village, 1920.

A Japanese postcard with the original caption "Airfield and aeroplane in Spasskoye", where you can see the blue-white-red stripes on the rudder and three-colour roundels on the lower wings of the 'American'. Military Aviation School of the Far East, Spasskoye village, 1920.

*LWF biplane code no. 36 and serial no. 12892.
Flown by kapitan Pleshkov, Manchurian Aviation Otryad.
Chita, August 1919.
Reconstruction by A. V. Kazakov*

Accepted in March 1919 at the Okeanskaya station of the Ussuri railway, the 18 'Americans' were distributed as follows: three went to the Far East Aviation School in Spasskoye village, three to Kurgan Aviation School and six each to the 14th and 15th Siberian Aviation Otryads.

At Kurgan the 'Americans' were assembled and flown. Later, Russian three-colour roundels were applied on the wings of the LWFs, while the three-colour stripes on the rudder were retained. Some of the machines retained the 'native' tactical numbers with the characteristic style of digits.

In July the 15th Otryad deployed to the front, while the 14th, which was to re-equip with Sopwiths, gave up its machines to the 15th and the Manchurian Aviation Otryads.

From the end of 1918 the Special Manchurian Unit (later Special, and then Consolidated Manchurian Division 'ataman Semënov') had an aviation detachment with a pair of decrepit aeroplanes. By the beginning of August 1919 the detachment had received no supplies from the 'avia-centre', until it was included in Kolchak's aviation under the name of "Manchurian Aviation Otryad". Two 'Americans', received from the 14th Siberian Otryad, constituted the entire equipment of the renewed aviation otryad.

After the defeat of Kolchak several machines were allocated to the aviation of the People's-Revolutionary Army (PRA) of the Far Eastern Republic (FER), and continued to serve until 1922.

In 1920 two 'Americans' found their way to the Moscow Central Aviation Park, where the strange machines were adorned with red five-pointed stars.

A train of a mobile aviation workshop of the PRA FER. The wagons carry Salmson no. 4514 of a defector pilot Ust'yantsev and a 'Sturtevant' with the 164 hp Benz engine, being despatched to Moscow. Wings with American recognition markings are visible. Summer 1920.

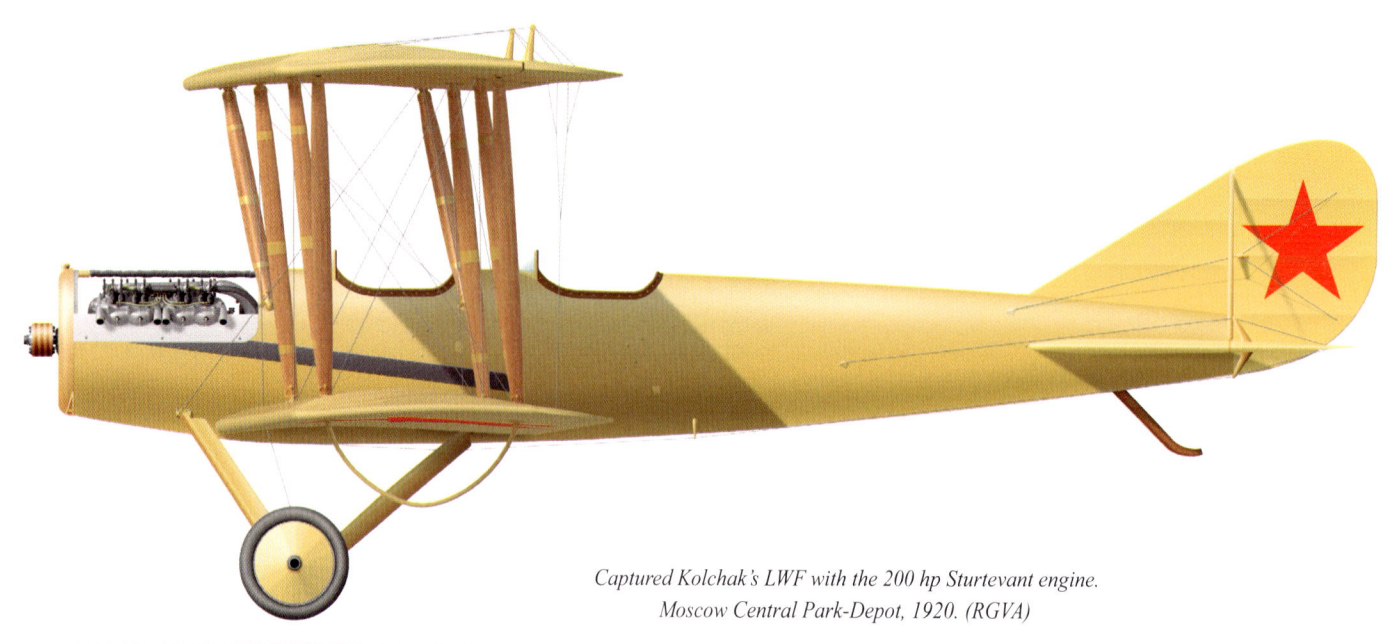

*Captured Kolchak's LWF with the 200 hp Sturtevant engine.
Moscow Central Park-Depot, 1920. (RGVA)*

In the Kurgan Military Aviation School, for example, a training aeroplane survived that was adorned with French and Russian recognition markings.

The 10th Aviation Otryad seems to have been the only unit of the entire aviation which had its own otryad insignia. This otryad's history dated back to the 10th Orenburg Otryad, which from January 1919 was completely re-formed and initially equipped with three Nieuport fighters. From June 1919 military pilot *shtabs-kapitan* G. I. Muromtsev became the commander of the 10th Otryad. In August the otryad was briefly withdrawn from the front line and sent to Omsk for replenishment and overhaul of its aeroplanes. The unit received two-seat Sopwiths, which will be discussed below.

Military pilot *praporshchik* A. V. Ryabov served with the 10th Otryad, having flown to the White side in August 1918 during the fighting for Kazan'. He has left memoirs, illustrated with beautiful photographs.[58]

---

[58] A. Riaboff. "Flying for the Czar", "Cross & Cockade" magazine, Vol. 11, No. 4/1970; A. Riaboff, Von Hardesty. "Reminiscences of a Russian Pilot. Gatchina Days.", Washington, D.C. Smithsonian Institution Press, 1986.

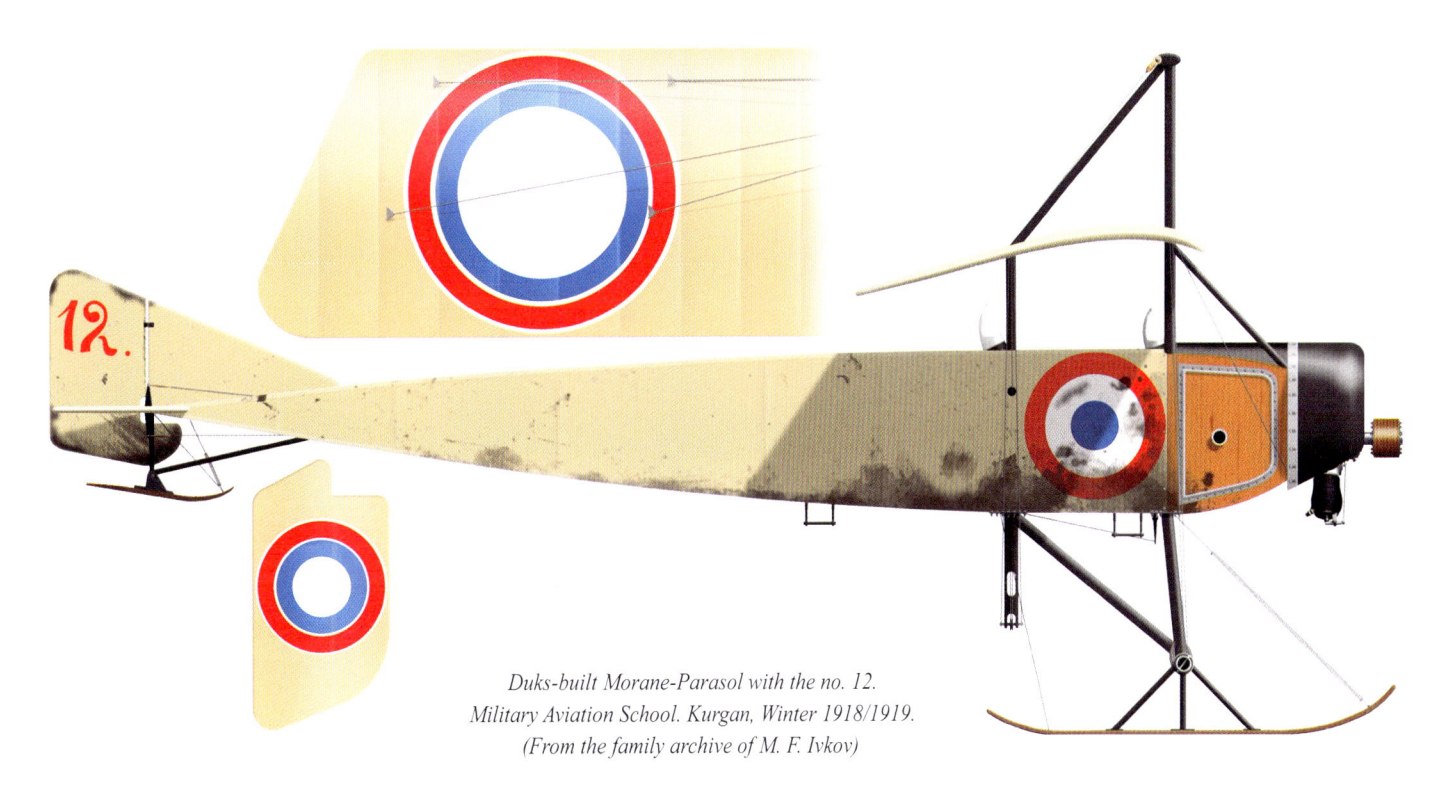

Duks-built Morane-Parasol with the no. 12.
Military Aviation School. Kurgan, Winter 1918/1919.
(From the family archive of M. F. Ivkov)

The rudders of all Nieuports were adorned with an emblem, a knight who saddled an eagle. The hero raised one hand to his eyes, peering into the distance, and held a sword and a flag in his other hand. There is no doubt that the heroic theme was directly connected with the surname of the commander of the 10th Aviation Otryad, *shtabs-kapitan* Muromtsev[59].

The otryad emblem probably started to be applied on the Nieuports no earlier than June 1919. It is rather difficult to date the picture that shows Ryabov posing with a Nieuport 17. In June and July the pilot flew reconnaissance sorties using various Nieuports, and after re-equipment of the otryad in Omsk he switched to a French Sopwith.

Another well-known photo of an aeroplane with the eagle-riding hero was taken in the summer of 1919. This Nieuport 23 was flown in combat by *praporshchik* Volkovoynov, who then moved on, like Ryabov, to a French Sopwith (although he did fly a Nieuport a couple of times).

---

[59] This Russian surname is derived from the name 'Muromets', which links with Il'ya Muromets, a hero of a well-known Russian tale (after whom Russian heavy bombers were called). (Translator's note)

*Assembling the aeroplanes of the 10th Aviation Otryad in workshops.
A Sopwith can be seen on the right.
One of the five Nieuports displays the otryad emblem.
Omsk. August 1919.*

*Praporshchik A. V. Ryabov, a pilot 10th Aviation Otryad, posing with
a French production Nieuport 17 fighter.
Summer 1919.*

Nieuport 17 with the emblem of the 10th Aviation Otryad. The machine is armed with a synchronised Vickers machine gun and is fitted with an additional fuel tank. 1919.

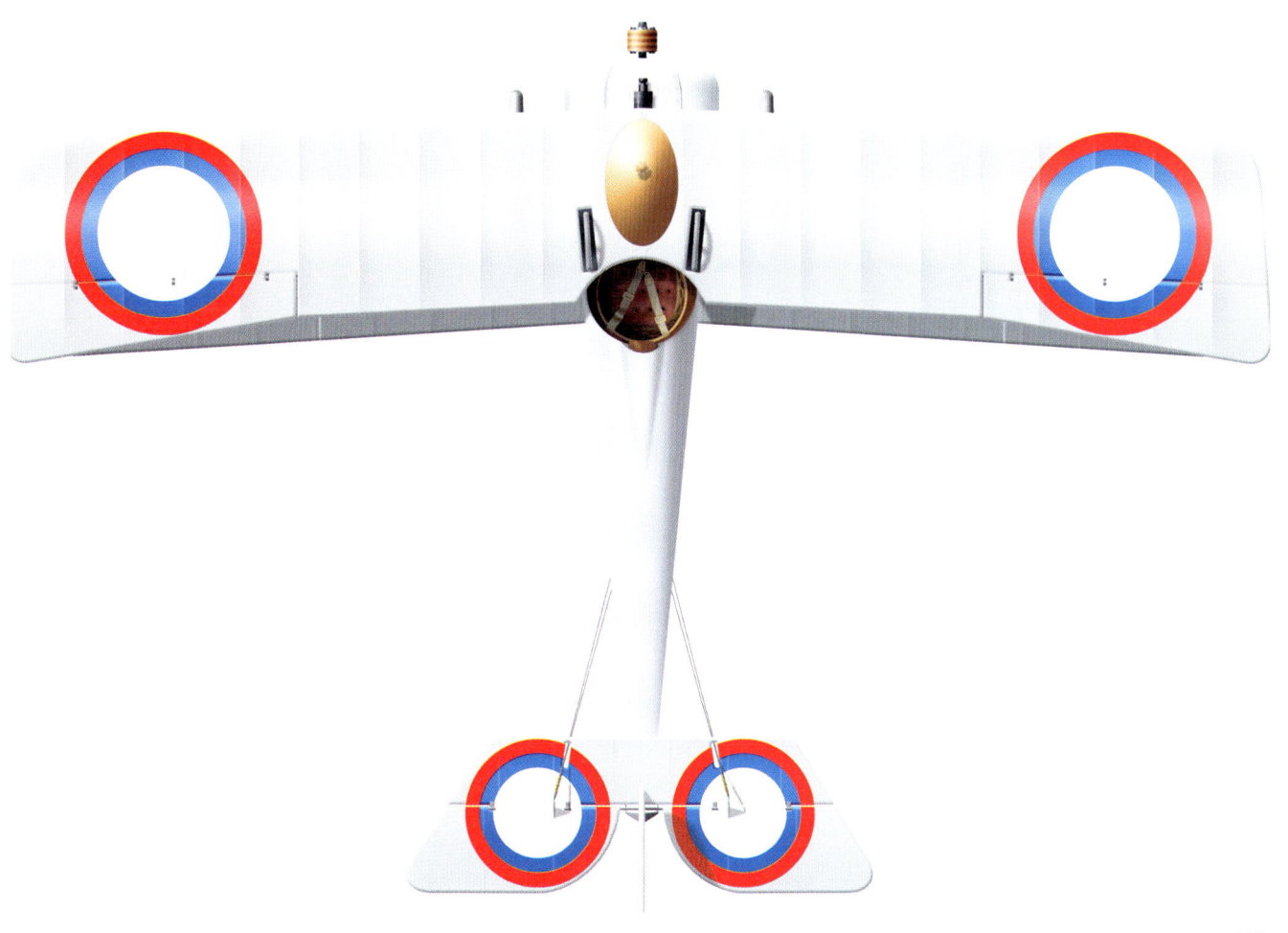

Nieuport 23 fighter flown by praporshchik M. A. Volkovoynov, 10th Aviation Otryad. Details of the otryad emblem on the rudder are slightly different from those on the Nieuport 17. 1919.

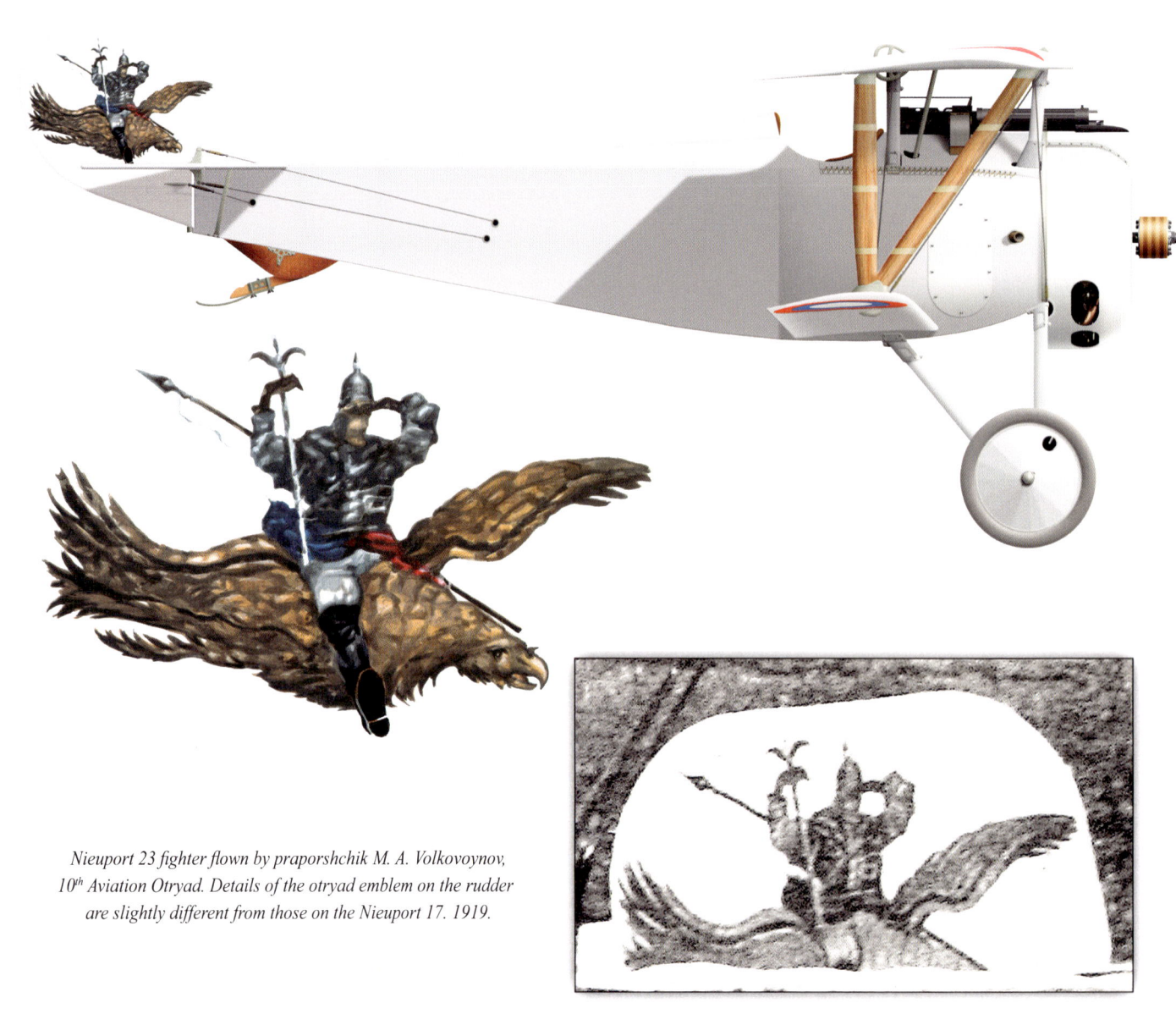

114

Photos from Ryabov's album show the 10th Aviation Otryad during the best period of its existence. Most were taken in early September 1919 at the airfield of the 3rd Army Aviation (6th and 10th Aviation Otryads) at Petropavlovsk during the fighting in the Kurgan area.

Ryabov's photographs captured all the machines of the otryad (three Sopwiths, a Nieuport 11, a Nieuport 17 and two of its three Nieuport 23s, and also a Morane-Parasol). It is noteworthy that the rudders of all the Nieuports are adorned with the otryad emblem. They are absent on the Sopwiths, and this can partly be explained by the fact that the 10th Otryad received the French aircraft at the front line.

The otryad's only Morane-Parasol, of *praporshchik* El'sner, which crashed on 12 September. The photo shows that the Russian flag was applied on its fuselage, rather than the Siberian white-green one, as it has been mistakenly interpreted earlier because of the poor quality of the photo.

In July 1919, two echelons with 15 Sopwiths arrived in Krasnoyarsk, earmarked to form two French aviation units for operations at the Siberian front. But in view of the fact that demobilisation of the French military mission in Siberia was soon declared, the Allies refused to form the units and all property was urgently transferred (sold) to Kolchak's aviation. Several Frenchmen under *Lieutenant* Amet managed to fight on the Eastern Front in August and even get some awards.[60] Then three Sopwiths were transferred to the 10th Aviation Otryad. The 6th Aviation Otryad also received the 'new' machines. Eight also went to the 3rd and 14th Siberian Otryads (three and five, respectively) at the end of August. During acceptance of the aeroplanes in Krasnoyarsk, *praporshchik* Gil'bikh, a pilot of the 14th Otryad, noted in the report:

On all aeroplanes wooden parts were covered with mould and metal ones with rust.[61]

In general, almost all the accepted Sopwiths underwent overhauls in the aircraft workshop in Omsk and reached the front line in September 1919.

In the pictures one of the Sopwiths of the 6th or 10th Aviation Otryad looks new and has Russian three-colour roundels on its planes. That is right: the 'Frenchman' had undergone an overhaul in the Omsk aircraft workshop and immediately went to the front line. One of the reports noted that:

because of their very bad condition, six machines were re-covered with fabric.[62]

Finally, let us consider the Sopwith flown by *praporshchik* Ryabov. The battered 'Frenchman' was painted in a camouflage colour, featured a three-colour pennant on its side, similar to the emblem of one of French *escadrilles*. French recognition markings were retained on the wings and rudder.

Sopwiths and Nieuports of the 10th Aviation Otryad at the Petropavlovsk airfield. September 1919.

60 For more details see the article "Frantsuzskiy otryad v armii Kolchaka" ("French unit in Kolchak's army") published in the anniversary collection "Krasnyy Vozdushnyy Flot. 1918–1923 gg." ("Red Air Force. 1918–1923"), Moscow. 1923. P. 52.
61 RGVA. F. 39499. Op. 1. D. 386. L. 67.
62 RGVA. F. 39499. Op. 1. D. 417. L. 58.

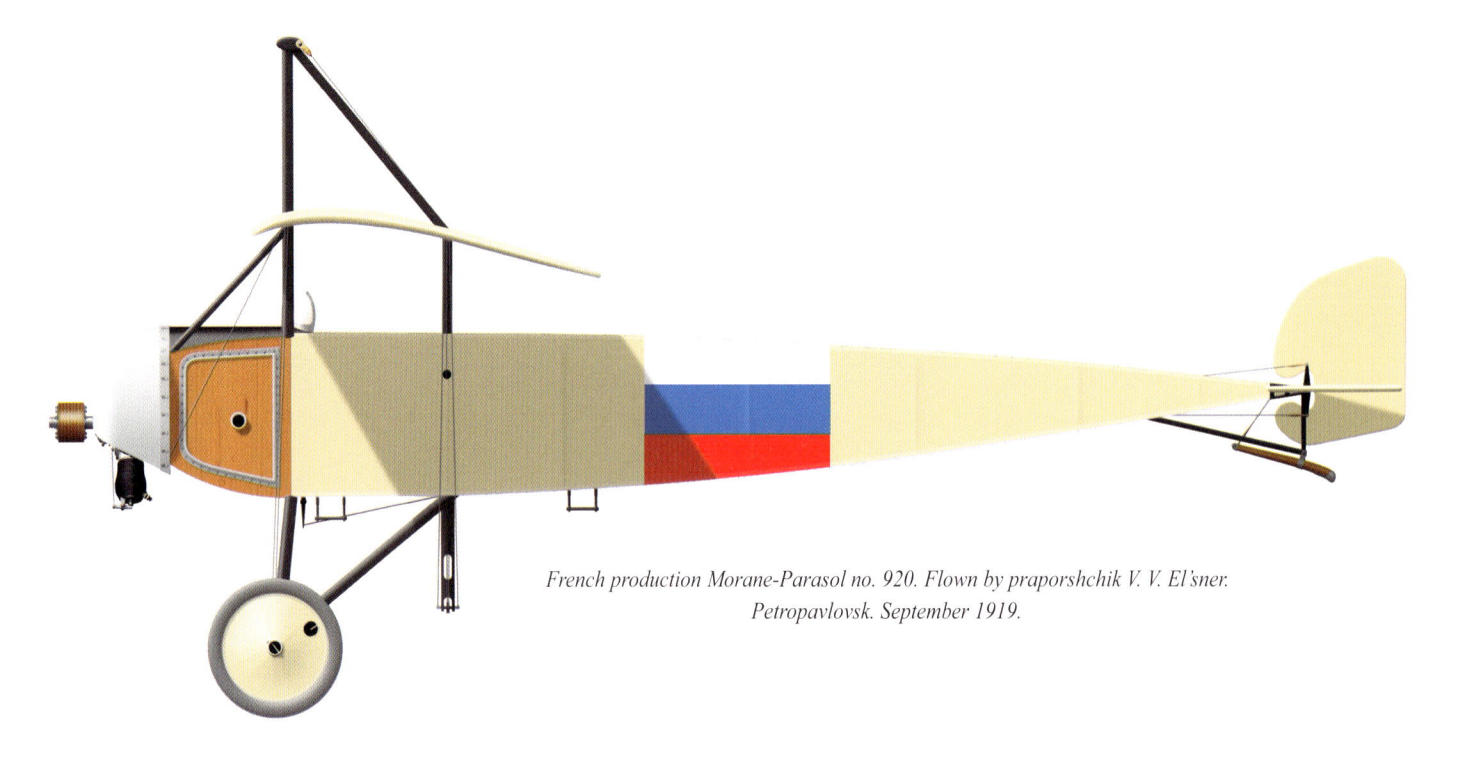

*French production Morane-Parasol no. 920. Flown by praporshchik V. V. El'sner.
Petropavlovsk. September 1919.*

*Airfield of the 10th and 6th Aviation Otryads.
Left to right: Sopwith 1½-Strutter, Morane-Parasol, Nieuport 11, Nieuport 23, Nieuport 17 or 23,
two Sopwith 1½-Strutters, a Nieuport and a Sopwith of the 6th Aviation Otryad.
Petropavlovsk, September 1919.*

Sopwith 1½-Strutter of the 3rd Army aviation (6th or 10th Aviation Otryad). Petropavlovsk, September 1919.

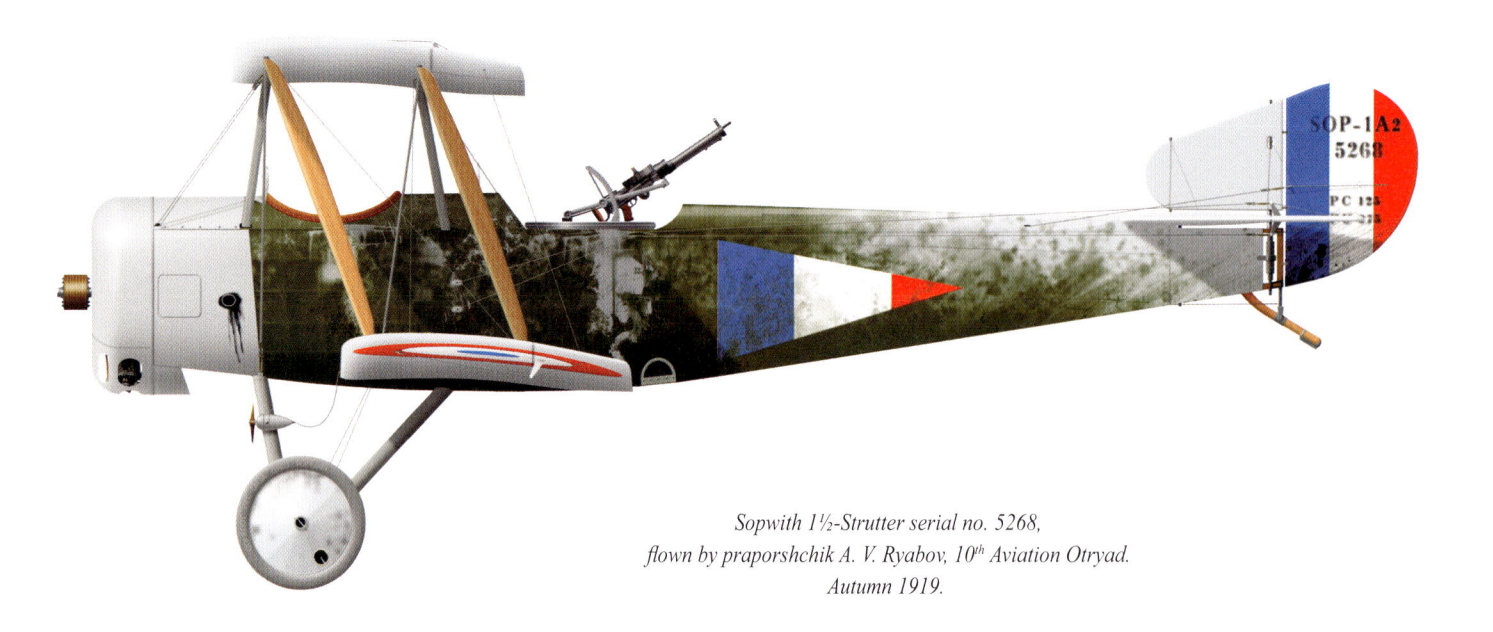

*Sopwith 1½-Strutter serial no. 5268,
flown by praporshchik A. V. Ryabov, 10th Aviation Otryad.
Autumn 1919.*

Flights in September-October 1919 in the area of Tyumen' and Kurgan were the last flash of activity of Kolchak's aviation, which retreated to the east, along with the remnants of ground units, under the onslaught of the Red troops.

At a critical period, when the Eastern aviation was living out its last days, orders were issued, not needed by anyone any more, to assign the name "Siberian" to all aviation otryads and even about new recognition markings that were never executed.

> In view of complaints from units [about] the difficulty of recognizing the existing recognition markings on our aeroplanes[,] the GenKvArmVost* has approved the following marking in addition to the existing three-colour roundels: two black crossed bands in the middle of the lower plane on the underside. The dimensions of the cross correspond to the width of the wing, and the width of the band is equal to one-fifth of its length. Three-colour roundel recognition markings remain in the previous place. NR14006. 23 Oct. 1919 Omsk**
>
> ** Quartermaster general of the Staff of the Supreme Commander of the Eastern Front armies*
> *** RGVA. F. 40025. Op. 1. D. 22. L. 171.*

Preparing a Sopwith 1½-Strutter for a combat sortie. Military pilot praporshchik Ryabov is in the cockpit and observer poruchik Moshkov receives bombs.
Petropavlovsk, Early September 1919.

On 22 December 1919 one of the last documents for Kolchak's aviation was issued, signed by the Commander of Air Force of the Eastern Front, *polkovnik* Samoylo:

> All aviation units of the front are diverted to Chita area for reforming and bringing up to combat condition. Announcing this, I ask for reports about the movement into Chita of the arriving echelon on 22 December this year at the Innokent'yevskaya No. 54 station, composed of my Department, HQ of the NachAviArm1, the 3rd and 14th [Siberian] Aviation Otryads, as well as the echelons that follow behind, of the 5th [Corps'], 6th and 10th Aviation Otryads, 1st and 2nd Aviation Workshops, HQ of the NachAviArm2 and 3, Central Aviation Park, Central Aviation Workshop, 1st, 2nd and 3rd Balloon Otryads.[63]

Only a small group of commanding staff and a few flyers managed to escape to the rear without being captured by the Reds. Thus ended the history of Kolchak's aviation.

63 RGVA. F. 39499. Op. 1. D. 334. L. 337.

Armed Forces of the Russian Eastern Periphery
(of ataman G. V. Semënov)

The period of the so-called Semënov's aviation began in 1920.

Salmsons and Spads had been ordered in France for the Russian troops in Siberia back in 1919, but by December only 25 Salmsons had arrived. These machines became the only type in Semënov's aviation.

French Salmson no. 423?. Military Aviation School of the Far East, Spasskoye village. Winter 1919/1920. (From the family archive of M. F. Ivkov)

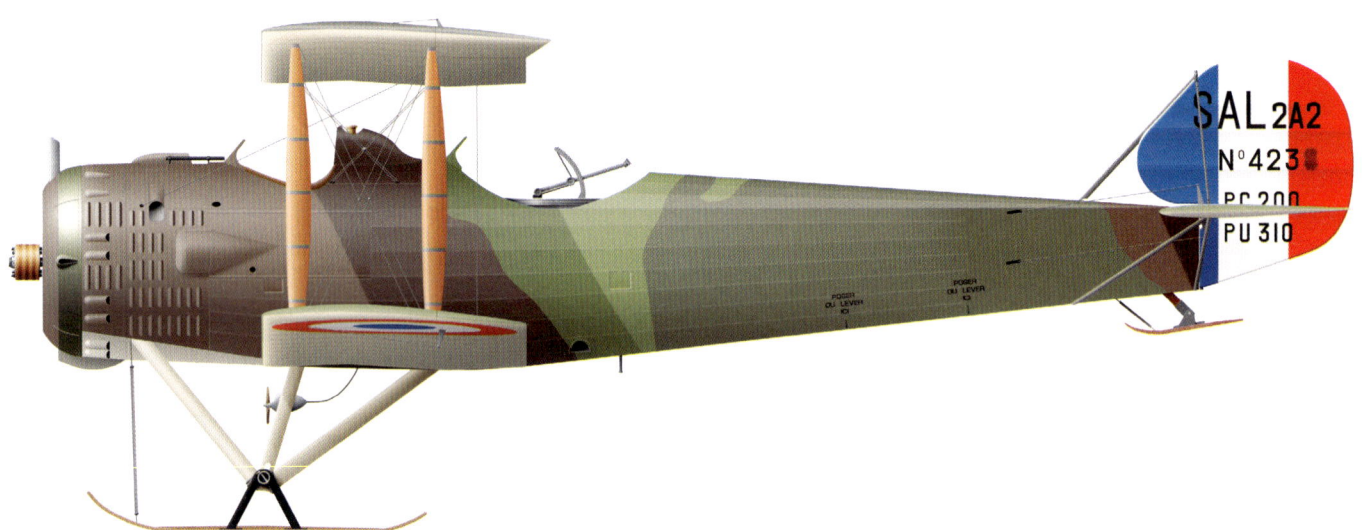

The following orders prove the organisation of two future Semënov's aviation otryads (except for the Manchurian one, which was in Chita).

**Orders of the Commander of the Land and Naval Forces
of the Provisional Government
No. 38**

29 February 1920 Fortress Vladivostok

I announce the decision of the Military Council of the Provisional Government of the Primor'ye region of Zemstvo authority of 26 February:

§ 1.
The Kurgan Military Aviation School is to be renamed the Military Aviation School of the Far East.

§ 2.
The Spasskaya Military Aviation School is to be disbanded, its property transferred to the Military Aviation School of the Far East, and the personnel transferred to the same school to fill in vacant posts (according to the establishment of the orders of the former Chief of Staff of the Commander-in-Chief of 30 April 1919 no. 396).

§ 4.
Aviation otryads nos. 1, 7, 8 and 9 are to be disbanded.

§ 5.
Re-forming of the aviation units is to be completed by 1 April of this year.

§ 6.
Aviation otryads nos. 1 and 2 are to be formed, subordinating them to the Head of the Military Aviation School of the Far East.

§ 7.
Military pilot Ivkov is appointed the Head of the Military Aviation School of the Far East, with the authority of a brigade commander.

§ 8.
The Head of the Military Aviation School of the Far East is operationally subordinated directly to the Head of the Land [and] Naval Forces, and in technical and economic matters to the Head of Engineering Supplies of the Authority of the Supreme Head of Supplies.

§ 10.
A reserve of aviation specialists is to be established at the Military Aviation School of the Far East.

Signed by: Comrade Chairman of the Military Council Lindberg, Secretary Bragin.

Commander of the Forces Krakovetskiy

Orders* to the Forces of the Russian Eastern Periphery

No. 66

24 March 1920 Chita city

The three formed aviation otryads are attached to and are at the disposal of:

Special Manchurian Aviation Otryad – Commander of the 1st Independent Army Corps;
1st Aviation Otryad – Quartermaster General of the Staff of the Commander of the Forces;
2nd Aviation Otryad – Commander of the 2nd Army Corps.

Commander of the Forces, General Staff, General-mayor Vojcechovský.

Chief of Staff, General Staff, General-mayor Shchepikhin.

* RGVA. F. 40294. Op. 1. D. 1. L. 38 s ob.

Thus, by April 1920, Semënov had three complete aviation otryads, equipped with French Salmsons. The otryads were part of the newly formed Far Eastern Army under *general-leytenant* Lokhvitskiy.

Photos of Semënov's aeroplanes of that period have not survived, except for a few, which do not show recognition markings, emblems or numbers.

A series of rare photos refers to the Manchurian Aviation Otryad.

Black eagles as recognition markings of Semënov's aviation were first mentioned in the orders to the forces of the Russian Eastern Front no. 186/a of 24 April 1920, signed by *general-mayor* Vojcechovský (Wojciechowski). The orders as such, with a drawing of the marking attached, have not been found yet, but a reference to these was found in another document.

Semënov's Salmson. Manchurian Aviation Otryad. Summer 1920.
(From the collection of M. Blinov)

O.M.O. shoulder emblem.
(From the collection of M. S. Selivanov)

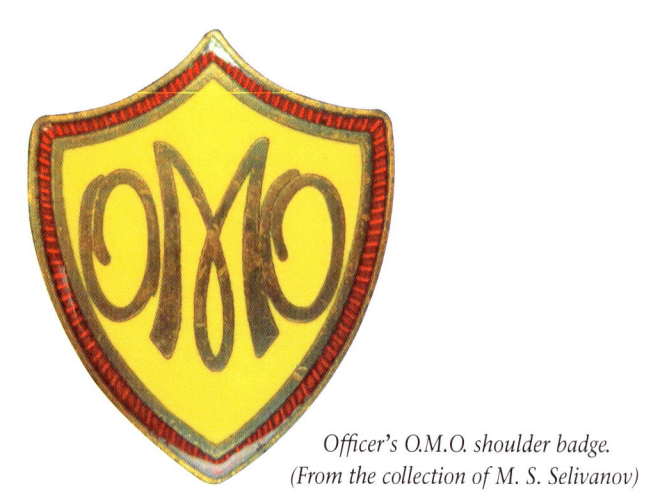

Officer's O.M.O. shoulder badge.
(From the collection of M. S. Selivanov)

Members of the Manchurian Aviation Otryad with the "O.M.O." shield (Osobyy Man'chzhurskiy Otryad or Special Manchurian Otryad) posing against a Salmson. Spring 1920

> **Orders* of the Asian Horse Division
> No. 105**
>
> 14th May 1920 Dauriya military town
>
> §5.
>
> By orders of the Commander of the Forces of the Russian Eastern Periphery of 24 April, no. 186/a, it is announced: in view of the fact that distinctive markings of our aeroplanes in most cases are all similar to those of the Reds, a new distinctive marking for our aeroplanes is introduced in the form of a black colour double-headed eagle, holding a propeller in his paws and two crossed swords. A drawing of the distinctive marking is attached to the orders.
>
> *For the head of the division
> polkovnik Kurenkov*
>
> RGVA. F. 39532. Op. 1. D. 29. L. 49.

The new recognition marking, with the exception of the second sword and the crown and other details, was clearly a copy of the 'black eagle', the shoulder strap brevet approved by the War Office orders no. 417 in 1913

for officers military pilots, serving in aviation otryads, rotas and schools. The insignia is superimposed, silver, dark-oxidised, represents a flying two-headed eagle with an airscrew and a sword in its paws and a bomb on the crossing of the airscrew and sword…[64]

*This shoulder strap military pilot brevet in 1913 version belonged to the commander of "Il'ya Muromets Kievskiy", I. S. Bashko.
(From the collection of M. A. Khainulin)*

The shoulder strap military pilot brevet without the crown, of the Provisional Government period, 1917.

The brevet without the crown or the monogram, aviation of the People's Army, 1918.

---

64   RGVIA. F. 2000. Op. 7. D. 62. L. 92.

Without a doubt, the double-headed eagle had no crown, and its appearance probably resembled the insignia of the Semënov period and the images on banknotes issued at the time. The royal monogram "H II" (Cyrillic for "N II") on the chest of the eagle may have been replaced with a shield with the abbreviation "O.M.O." (*Osobyy Man'chzhurskiy Otryad* or Special Manchurian Otryad) or "A.S." (Cyrillic for "Ataman Semënov").

O.M.O. badge, Harbin, 1921.
(From the collection of M. S. Selivanov)

O.M.O. badge, 1932.
(From the collection of M. S. Selivanov)

Recognition marking on Semënov's aeroplanes in accordance with the orders no. 185/a of 24 April 1920. Reconstruction by A. V. Kazakov

The treasury bill of 100 roubles of the Government of the Russian Eastern Periphery 1920, never released into circulation, decorated with the two-headed eagle of the Provisional Government

A mass flight of Semënov's pilots to the side of the Reds took place on 20 July 1920. Thanks to Dedyulin's testimony, unique details about the recognition markings of Ataman Semënov's aviation have been preserved.

Testimony* of the defector pilot Dedyulin

[...]

20 July [1920] – I [Dedyulin], military pilot Kruchinskiy, naval pilot Agapov, military pilot Balyagin and passenger Abramov flew to the side of the Reds in Salmson aeroplanes.

[...]

Information about the enemy, Semënov's aviation
Head of Aviation-Automobile Units – military pilot *Polkovnik* Makarov, assistant – military pilot *kapitan* Astaf'yev, Chita city.

1st Aviation Otryad
Remaining: Head – military pilot *kapitan* Tikhomirov. Military pilot podporuchik Mozhevetinov. Observers: Kondry, *kornet* Apraksin, *yesaul* Kruchinin, *praporshchik* Solov'yëv. One Salmson (unserviceable, engine) remains in the otryad. Command 60–80 people. Two railway cars of petrol in cans. Otryad left Chita on 18 July 1920 to the Borzya station. Distinctive markings on the lower planes "**black double-headed eagles**".

2nd Aviation Otryad
Head – military pilot *podpolkovnik* Kachurin. Military pilot *kapitan* Slyusarenko. Military pilot (name and title I don't remember). Aeroplanes: two serviceable and one unserviceable (engine). On 10 July the otryad arrived from Nerchinsk to Borzya station.

Special Manchurian Aviation Otryad
More reliable and exclusively Semënov's otryad. Commander – military pilot *podpolkovnik* Pleshkov. 4 pilots (Shishkovskiy, I don't remember the others). 4 observers. 4 machines – serviceable. Was at the Borzya station.

Japanese Aviation
In Chita, there are otryads (Salmson, Sopwiths and Farman XXX). It is characteristic that with a slightest damage the machines are not repaired by the Japanese, but are burned, leaving only the engine. From Chita, the Japanese aviation should go to Spasskoye. Pilots and observers 5-6 people each, fly poorly compared to ours. Distinctive marking "red disc" (sun) on the lower and upper planes and on the rudder. In Spasskoye a Japanese aviation otryad, 8–9 Sopwiths single-seaters, 5–6 pilots, 5–6 observers.

[...]

The rest of the aviation in the East
1st Red Aviation Otryad in Khabarovsk, detached from the Far East school, composed of one Salmson, two "Americans" and one Morane-Parasol. Commander – military pilot Naydënov, military pilot Sinel'nikov, French pilot Bykhovskiy and 4 names I don't remember, 4 observers. The otryad is well supplied, based in Blagoveshchensk with comrade Shilov and combat-ready.

Far East school
Currently doesn't work. 15 people that arrived from France were in a revolutionary mood – joining partisan otryads. As a military booty the aviation school has not worked after 5 April. There were: Farman IV – 5; Farman XX, Farman XVI, Morane G – 2 of each; Morane-Parasol – 3; Farman VII, Farman XXII, Lebed', Voisin, "American", Nieuport 21, Farman 30 – one of each. Crashed: Salmson, "American", two Farman IVs and 3–4 Morane-Parasols and Morane Gs. No recognition markings on training machines.

Spasskaya school
Actually doesn't work, no pupils have graduated. Head – Staripavlov, included in Semënov's reserve of aviation specialists and lives in Harbin. Previously, the property that used to be in the Spasskaya school was transferred to the Far East school.

[...]

Interrogation was carried out by temp. acting military commissar of the Air Force of Siberia Lepilov. Sent on 20 August 1920 to the military commissar of the Staff of the AF of the Republic.

* *RGVA. F. 39454. Op. 1. D. 7. D. 139ob.*

The White movement in the east of Russia suffered defeat after defeat under the onslaught of the Red troops. The army could no longer maintain three otryads, and the first two were merged into one – "Army Aviation Otryad of the Far Eastern Army".

> **Orders***
> **to the forces of the Far Eastern Army**
> **No. 444**
>
> "15" September 1920 Chita station
>
> In order to make the aviation units more efficient, I order:
>
> 1) The first and second aviation otryads to be combined into one aviation otryad with adoption of the name: **"Army Aviation Otryad of the Far Eastern Army"**.
>
> 2) The staff and technical equipment that exceed the establishment to be assigned to other aviation and automobile units, by orders of the Head of Aviation-Automobile Units.
>
> 3) Appoint an experienced military pilot as the commander of the combined Army Aviation Otryad, by orders of the Head of Aviation-Automobile Units.
>
> 4) Complete the combining of units within a week.
>
> *General-leytenant Verzhbitskiy*
>
> * RGVA. F. 29. Op. 2. D. 103. L. 72–73.

Memories of the 2nd Aviation Otryad commander, rotmistr V. A. Zinov'yev survive:

Upon arrival we had not even had the time to report this to the headquarters, when a report was received from the Head of the Manchurian Division, general Nechayev, that the Reds had already started attacking him from the direction of Makkaveyevo, attacks which they have so far successfully repelled, telegraph communication with the Orenburg troops was already interrupted. According to rumours, they have cleared the station and moved to the south. Scouts of the Reds appeared at the Peschanka station. In all likelihood, the Reds were well aware that at this time the ataman and his staff were in Chita, and so they hurried to cut it off and capture it. Then it was decided that the ataman would fly in our machine to Dauriya. Since our machine was a two-seater, Salmson type, the ataman flew with my commander next day, that is 20 October, from Chita and on the same day safely landed after 3 hours and 10 minutes at Dauriya station, having flown about 500 kilometres.[65]

The ataman himself recalled this flight:

At the persistent invitation of the army commander general Verzhbitskiy, at the end of October 1920 I went to Chita for a meeting on the matter of further negotiations with Verkhneudinsk. I arrived there in an armoured train and stayed in Chita in it. At night I was awakened by the head of the Chita garrison, general Bangerski, who informed me that the Reds suddenly attacked the railway line near the Karymskaya station, captured that station and thoroughly destroyed the tracks and a fairly significant bridge across the river Ingoda near the station. Armoured trains and units of the Manchurian Division were urgently thrown into the breakthrough and fought against superior forces of the Reds.
Then I received a report from my counter-intelligence that Vinogradov, a member of the People's Assembly of the Trans-Baikal region, with the consent of the army headquarters, is negotiating with the Verkhneudinsk government about the capitulation of the army, one of the conditions of which was my arrest and extradition to the Reds.
Seeing that I cannot count on the army headquarters and units of the 2nd and 3rd Corps', and not having any of my core units around me, except for the armoured train, which was completely useless in the current situation, I was forced to fly on an airplane to Dauriya, where I was expected by units of the 1st Corps of general-leytenant Matsiyevskiy, who had replaced general-leytenant D. F. Semënov as the commander of the corps.
The aeroplane, flown by polkovnik Kachurin, was unserviceable, and during the entire flight, which lasted two hours and fifteen minutes, a mechanic at my feet was soldering the petrol tank.[66]

---

65   GA RF. F. 5881. Op. 2. D. 357. L. 20.
66   Semënov G. M. "O sebe: Vospominaniya, mysli i vyvody / Ataman Semënov" ("About myself: Memoirs, thoughts and conclusions / Ataman Semënov"). M: OOO "Izdatel'stvo ACT", 2002. p. 241.

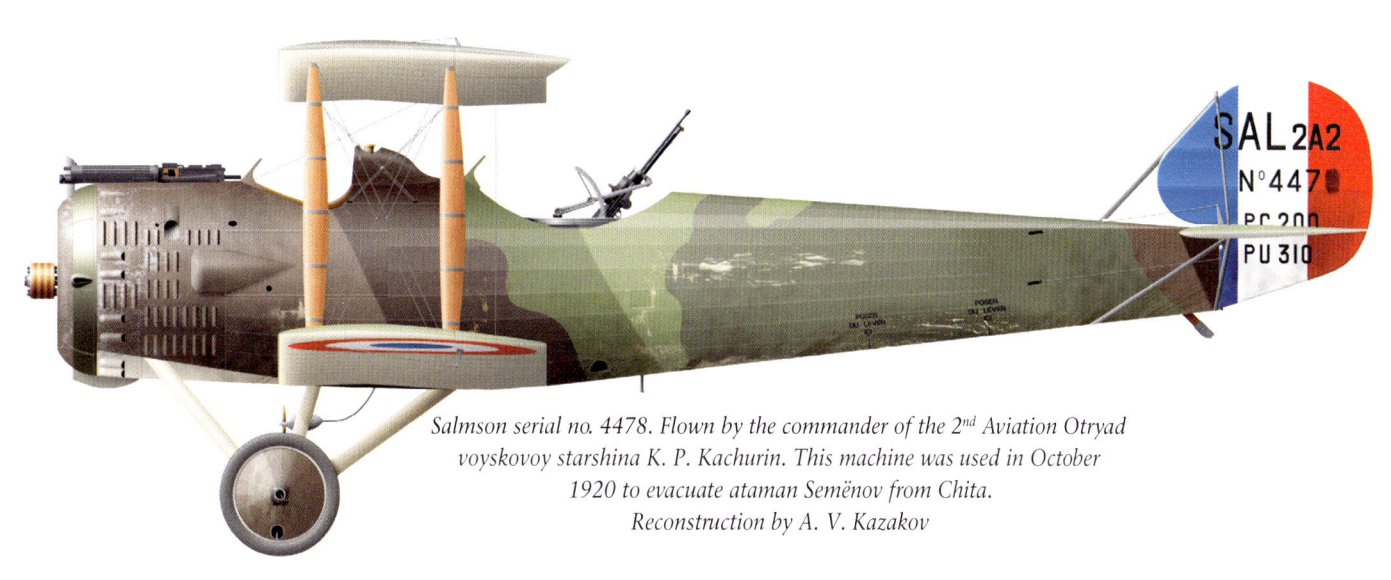

Salmson serial no. 4478. Flown by the commander of the 2nd Aviation Otryad voyskovoy starshina K. P. Kachurin. This machine was used in October 1920 to evacuate ataman Semënov from Chita. Reconstruction by A. V. Kazakov

In the autumn of 1920, Semënov's aviation was living its last days. Chita fell, the troops of the Far Eastern Army retreated to the Dauriya station, that is to Manchurian territory. The battle for Trans-Baikal was completely lost.

Orders*
to the forces of the Far Eastern Army
No. 531

10 November 1920 Dauriya station

§1.

1. Manchurian Aviation Otryad 'Ataman Semënov' to be disbanded.
2. Machines to be transferred to the Army Aviation Otryad.
3. The staff and all technical equipment to be assigned to other aviation and automobile units, by orders of the Head of Aviation-Automobile Units.

General-leytenant Verzhbitskiy

* RGVA. F. 39729. Op. 1. D. 4. L. 206.

The orders to disband the Manchurian Aviation Otryad were clearly late: after leaving Dauriya and Matsiyevskaya by 20 November 1920 there were no aeroplanes left whatsoever. Some had been burnt, and some captured by the Reds.

A Salmson of the 1st Insurgent Amurskiy Aviation Otryad. This machine was previously used in the Military Aviation School of the Far East. Winter 1920/1921. The original caption reads "Bikin station. Before the flight to Spassk". (TsMVS)

The story of Semënov's aviation of 1920 does not end the history of the aviation of the White forces in the east of Russia. During 1921–1922 the aviation was represented in the form of HQs and detachments with various military formations. The presence of aircraft is extremely rarely mentioned in surviving documents.

Remains of the Far Eastern army moved with great difficulty to Primor'ye. Units were split into 'Kappelevtsy' and 'Semënovtsy'. The latter did not recognise the authority of the Priamurskiy Provisional Government of S. D. Merkulov, formed in Vladivostok in May 1921. In Grodekovo, the troops that were reporting to ataman Semënov formed the Grodekovo group under *general-mayor* Savel'yev, which in September eventually became subordinated to the Priamurskiy Provisional Government. For example, the headquarters of the group included the authority of the head of aviation (most likely the former authority of the head of aviation of the Far Eastern Army).

The 2nd Siberian Rifle Corps under *general-mayor* I. S. Smolin ('Kappelevtsy') was located in Nikol'sko-Ussuriysk. As of 28 July 1921, the corps included the "Combined Group of Aviation-Automobile Units" (4 junior commissioned officers, 16 non-commissioned officers, 7 operational and 6 non-operational soldiers, 7 cart horses and 2 horse-carts)[67].

The Spassk garrison (*general-mayor* Bordzilovskiy) included a Military Aviation School under *shtabs-kapitan* Bazanov (231 people, 5 automobiles, 1 field kitchen, no armament).[68]

In this form the school continued to exist throughout 1922. It is known that it included about ten training machines and flying training even continued.

In August 1921 an "Automobile-Aviation Unit" (from March 1922 "Automobile-Aviation Unit of the Fortress Engineering HQ") under *podpolkovnik* Pestov was formed at the HQ of the Head of the Engineers of the Vladivostok fortress. The unit controlled an automobile workshop, aviation and automobile depots of the Priamurskiy government forces.

In June 1922 *general-leytenant* M. K. Diterikhs became the commander of all the armed forces of the Far East and the ruler of the Priamurskiy Zemskiy kray. In August Diterikhs was declared Voevoda, and the forces of the Priamurskiy government were renamed the Zemskaya Rat'. The newly formed headquarters did not include an aviation HQ. Only an Automobile-Aviation Unit under Pestov continued to exist. In September, when active hostilities resumed, the Order of Battle of the Zemskaya Rat' included: 6,228 bayonets, 1,684 sabres, 81 machine guns, 24 guns and 4 armoured trains.[69]

As of 1 October 1922 the Povolzhskaya group of *general-mayor* V. M. Molchanov included an "Aviation otryad" under *praporshchik* A. A. Rozhdestvenskiy (three aeroplanes: Salmson, LWF and Nieuport 21).[70] The Military Air School of the Far East was also reporting to the Zemskaya Rat'.[71]

In November 1922, after the fall of Spassk and the crossing of the Chinese border by the Zemskaya Rat' forces, the history of the White forces' aviation of the Russian Civil War came to a close.

---

67 RGVA. F. 40151. Op. 1. D. 7. L. 284.
68 RGVA. F. 40151. Op. 1. D. 6. L. 19b.
69 Shishkin S. N. "Grazhdanskaya voyna na Dal'nem Vostoke" ("Civil War in the Far East"). M.: Voyenizdat. 1957. p. 244.
70 Ryzhov I. L. "Posledniy pokhod: Zaklyuchitel'nyy etap Grazhdanskoy voyny v Rossii (sentyabr'—oktyabr' 1922 goda v Primor'ye)" ("The Last Advance: The closing stage of the Civil War in Russia (September–October 1922 in Primor'ye)". Vladivostok, "Dal'nauka", 2013. p. 23.
71 RGVA. F. 40189. Op. 1. D. 7. L. 35 s ob.